OXBOW INSIGHTS IN ARCHAEOLOGY

FIRST LIGHT
The Origins of Newgrange

Robert Hensey

D0937543

Oxbow Books
Oxford & Philadelphia

Published in the United Kingdom in 2015 by

OXBOW BOOKS
10 Hythe Bridge Street, Oxford OX1 2EW

and in the United States by

OXBOW BOOKS
908 Darby Road, Havertown, PA 19083

Paperback Edition: ISBN 978-1-78297-951-7
Digital Edition: ISBN 978-1-78297-952-4

A CIP record for this book is available from the British Library

Printed in the United Kingdom by Short Run Press, Exeter

For a complete list of Oxbow titles, please contact:

United Kingdom	United States of America
Oxbow Books	Oxbow Books
Telephone (01865) 241249	Telephone (800) 791-9354
Fax (01865) 794449	Fax (610) 853-9146
Email: oxbow@oxbowbooks.com	Email: queries@casemateacademic.com
www.oxbowbooks.com	www.casemateacademic.com/oxbow

Oxbow Books is part of the Casemate group

Front cover: Photograph courtesy of Robert Ardill, www.IrelandUpClose.com.

I prefer winter and fall, when you feel the bone structure of the landscape ... Something waits beneath it, the whole story doesn't show.

Andrew Wyeth (1965)

What happens when a new work of art is created is something that happens simultaneously to all the works of art which preceded it. The existing monuments form an ideal order among themselves, which is modified by the introduction of the new (the really new) work of art among them. The existing order is complete before the new work arrives; for order to persist after the supervention of novelty, the whole existing order must be, if ever so slightly, altered; and so the relations, proportions, values of each work ... toward the whole are readjusted; and this is conformity between the old and the new.

T. S. Eliot (1921)

Contents

Preface   vii
Acknowledgements   x
List of Illustrations   xiii

Introduction   1

1.   The Earliest Irish Passage Tombs   10

2.   Constructing New Realities   29

3.   Into the Earth   50

4.   Waiting for the Sun   66

5.   Where the River Meets the Sea   79

6.   Going Public   95

7.   A Secret History   119

8.   Journey to Newgrange   137

Conclusion: An Archaeology of the Otherworld   155

Notes   160
References   171
Index   189

Schematic illustration of three types of passage tomb (to scale).

Preface

I remember the first time I entered Newgrange. Taking in its great splendour and having no response but to laugh at the impossibility of it all. Two hundred thousand tonnes of stone all told, so ancient, and yet, science fiction-like, designed to allow the entry of a narrow beam of winter solstice light. What was it for? Where could such skill, such extraordinary ambition have come from?

I once had a Shakespeare lecturer, a well-known dramatist in his own right, who engaged his classes' attention by announcing he would impart the secrets to understanding King Lear. Pacing across the vast stage of the *Aula Maxima* he proclaimed in front of the four hundred eager students – pens alert on their first day to make sure any crucial information was not left unrecorded – that "To understand King Lear one has to" – *dramatic pause* – "first know Hamlet". He continued, "To understand Hamlet one has to" – *dramatic pause* – "know Richard III". And so it went, after each dramatic pause, he listed another famous Shakespearean play – until the students got the point.

Such is the case with archaeology, too. There is, I believe, a kind of knowledge that can be acquired through examining a great many related sites, seeing them at different times of year, in different weather conditions, from different perspectives. One can slowly take in subtle details of a monument or place, sometimes unconsciously. This 'soft knowledge' compliments and informs the hard knowledge that is the conventional goal and output of archaeological work. For instance, one could observe a slightly unusual tilt of a capstone not present at other sites and know, instinctively, it has been moved in the past, perhaps pushed aside in the course of antiquarian investigations and clumsily replaced. Observing poorly completed work and mistakes from the past can also be illuminating, sometimes allowing our ancient ancestors, with all their human frailties, to be imagined; one might sense the frustration of the Neolithic artist who could not quite fashion a successful double-spiral that another carver made so perfectly on a nearby kerbstone. Conversely, observing a clever architectural improvement or structural addition to a monument can allow a glimpse into the mind and working processes of the monument builders, an insight into their aims and successes. For instance, the way in which the cleverly designed roof-box at Newgrange offsets the rise of the hill on which the monument was built by directing the winter solstice sunlight through the elevated roof-box two metres above the floor of the passage entrance and so directly into the chamber (Plate 5).

At the time of that first visit to Newgrange I was only dimly aware of similar sites in the west of Ireland, less sophisticated equivalents, but few or no information or publications on those monuments were readily available in the public sphere. Then in mid-1990s as the Internet was becoming more utilised, discoveries from the second campaign of excavations at the Carrowmore passage tomb complex, County Sligo (and intriguingly early dates) were placed online. The speed at which information from those excavations was released seemed almost instantaneous compared with the usual pace of archaeological publication. The excitement around the Carrowmore work and findings encouraged me to visit the site, and subsequently similar monuments in the west of Ireland and nationally. As I became familiar with greater numbers of passage tombs, I came to believe that the monuments outside of the Boyne Valley possessed valuable pieces of the Newgrange puzzle. Each new site studied changed and deepened ones understanding. Not that one needs personal experience of every passage tomb on the island, but after many years considering these monuments I came to the conclusion that Newgrange cannot be comprehended without an in-depth knowledge of at least all four major passage tomb complexes (which between them contain approximately half of all Irish passage tombs).

As I have attempted to show in this book, especially in the opening chapters, the most westerly cluster at Carrowmore has a particularly important role in understanding the history of the Irish passage tomb tradition in Ireland, but so too do the monuments at the other major complexes, and not least the other monuments which neighbour Newgrange within the Brú na Bóinne complex. When considered as a group, the passage tombs of Ireland can also provide unexpected insights into the beliefs, concerns and religious activities of communities in the Neolithic not apparent when a single monument is examined in isolation. Ultimately, Newgrange is a materialisation of a lengthy evolution of the beliefs and thought-worlds of the communities which constructed passage tombs through time.

As is the case for many authors, in hindsight I realise I have written the book I wanted to read at the beginning of this journey, after that first visit to Newgrange, one that could begin to address where Newgrange came from, why it is there at all.

Acknowledgements

Many people have helped me to bring this book to fruition. I am especially grateful to those individuals who read all or parts of it. Elizabeth Shee Twohig was brave enough to read a very rough draft of the manuscript and provided many useful suggestions. Conor Brady read the text through on more than one occasion; his encouragement and detailed comments were immensely valuable at an important stage in the process. Frank Prendergast kindly fact-checked Chapter Four. Clare Tuffy suggested some useful corrections to my account of the winter solstice event at Newgrange, and generally reassured me that my memory has not completely gone (yet). William Roche fact-checked information about the life cycle of the salmon and the salmon runs on the Boyne for Chapter Five. Dave Wall examined the Knowth carving and provided information on humpback whale prevalence in the past. A few kind souls with no connection to the world of archaeology were patient enough to proofread the text – thanks especially to Susan and Lauren. Finally, Padraig Meehan and Marion Dowd read and re-read drafts of this work in its various incarnations; I cannot be completely sure it would exist without their support over several years.

I am indebted to colleagues who have given of their time and expertise for everything from a vital reply to some obscure query, to making available previously unpublished or otherwise difficult to access material: Stefan Bergh, Conor Brady, Clive Burrows, Neil Carlin, Joe Fenwick, Carleton Jones, Ann Lynch, Frances Lynch, Ian Meehan, Sam Moore, Muiris O'Sullivan, Frank Prendergast, Rick Schulting, Colin Richards, Guillaume Robin, Chris Scarre, George Sevastopulo, Elizabeth Shee Twohig, Alison Sheridan, Geraldine Stout, Julian Thomas and John Waddell. To all these I am extremely thankful. I would particularly like to thank Ann Lynch for making available to me unpublished information from her important excavations at Newgrange. Some of the material in this book has been published previously in the *Oxford Journal of Archaeology*, *Time and Mind*, *Préhistoires Méditerranéenes* and the *Neolithic Studies Group Seminar Papers, Volume 13*.

Clare Tuffy, manager of the Brú na Bóinne Visitor Centre, has always been tremendously supportive. For many of us Newgrange would not be quite the place or experience it is today without Clare's warmth and enthusiasm. The Office of Public Works was very accommodating in granting me access to the chambers at Knowth in the course of my PhD. The National Museum of Ireland has been extremely helpful in facilitating visits to their collection for all research and projects undertaken there in the last ten years, not least the Carrowmore Pins Project with Stefan Bergh. Stefan has provided stalwart advice through several stages of my academic career, not least through my doctoral work, and our subsequent work together has always been a pleasure. Thanks are owed to William Roche and Paddy Gargan senior research officers with Inland Fisheries Ireland, and Robert Bergin, bailiff on the Boyne River, for information about the life cycle of the Atlantic salmon and the Boyne River salmon runs.

Ken Williams kindly gave permission to use several of his magnificent photographs; if the book is a visual success it will be due in no small part to Ken's photography. Robert Ardill of www. IrelandUpClose provided the cover photograph. The National Museum of Ireland gave permission to use two photographs of finds from Carrowmore (taken by photographer Bryan Routledge). Breda McWalter and the OPW kindly provided permission to the Newgrange access tunnel above the passage for the photographs in Plate 8. Thanks to Con Brogan of the Photographic Unit of National Monuments for permission to use his spectacular aerial image of Carrowkeel. Tony McMahon of the Photographic Unit was also extremely helpful. I would like to acknowledge Sligo County Library for permission to use the W. F. Wakeman sketch of Heapstown Cairn. Paul Kelly went out of his way to find specific pictures of Newgrange, though unfortunately

I could not use those images in the end. Guillaume Robin helped create the generic image of three types of passage tomb, and gave permission to use several of the illustrations from his superb PhD and book on passage tomb art. Elizabeth Shee Twohig kindly sourced an original photograph from the O'Kelly excavations. Paul O'Conner did preliminary work on the Knowth West graphic. Padraig Meehan fired-up his monster computers for assistance with graphic work. Many writers permitted me to reproduce their published illustrations. I would like to thank Gabriel Cooney, George Eogan, Guillaume Robin and Harvey Whitehouse. The Tate Modern and Olafur Eliasson kindly granted permission to reproduce a photograph of 'The weather Project' from the stunning 2003 exhibition in the Turbine Hall. Finally, special thanks to Eve O'Kelly and family for allowing use of images by M. J. and Claire O'Kelly.

I am sincerely grateful to Oxbow Books for their care and attention to this project, particularly publishing director Clare Litt. Prof. Richard Bradley has given me tremendous personal and professional support when most needed, not least in encouraging me to write this book. Richard and many other people – too many to name – have influenced my thinking on Newgrange and the Neolithic period since the subject first began to fascinate me many years ago. My thanks to all. Lastly, I am forever indebted to my wife Lauren for her patience and perseverance during the completion of this book.

List of Illustrations

Plates

Frontispiece: Schematic illustration of three types of passage tomb.

1. Newgrange from the south with Site B in the foreground.
2. Lemnaghbeg Type 1 passage tomb, Co. Antrim.
3. *Above*: Cairn I, Loughcrew with Cairn T in the distance.
   Below: Cairn K, Carrowkeel.
4. Orthostat L19, Newgrange.
5. *Above*: Winter solstice sunlight entering Newgrange.
   Below: Path of solstice light.
6. 'The Weather Project', Olafur Eliasson.
7. Knowth West chamber art.
8. *Above*: Hidden art on roof-box 'back corbel', Newgrange.
   Below: Deeply carved rainwater groove on roofslab 3 above the passage at Newgrange.

Table

3.1. Modes of religiosity contrasted.

Figures

0.1. Grooves cut into the upper faces of roofstones to channel water away from the structure.
1.1. Brú na Bóinne passage tombs and related monuments.
1.2. Schematic map of main passage tomb locations in Ireland.
1.3. Passage tomb pins.
1.4. Carrowmore 3.
1.5. Ballintoy passage tomb.
2.1. Covered passage, Slieve Gullion.
2.2. Cairns G and H, Carrowkeel.

2.3. Corbelled roof, Cairn T, Loughcrew.

2.4. A selection of passage tombs with emphasis on the right-hand side.

2.5. Orthostat 45, Knowth West.

3.1. Cairn F, Carrowkeel.

3.2. Author inside a passage tomb recess, Cairn G, Carrowkeel.

3.3. Incised lines and deeper carving, Knowth West.

4.1. Beam of sunlight entering Cairn G, Carrowkeel.

4.2. Roof-box at Newgrange.

5.1. Materials transported to Newgrange.

5.2. Whalebone objects from Carrowmore.

5.3. Close-up of art from the chamber of the western tomb at Knowth with outline of possible humpback whale carving.

5.4. Humpback whale.

6.1. Stone balls of varying scales from Loughcrew.

6.2. Ovoid macehead, Knowth East.

6.3. Basin stones from the east recess at Newgrange.

6.4. Queen Maeve's tomb.

6.5. Heapstown Cairn.

7.1. Hidden art on inner face of kerbstone (K13) at Newgrange.

7.2. Orthostats from Newgrange and Knowth with art occurring beneath ground level.

7.3. East recess roofstone art, Newgrange. Note areas of occluded art.

7.4. Newgrange entrance stone, K1.

7.5. Newgrange plan and elevation.

8.1. Carrowmore 7 with Queen Maeve's tomb in the background.

8.2. The Carrowkeel passage tomb complex.

8.3. Loughcrew Cairn T with Cairn S in the foreground.

Introduction

Newgrange is one of an elite group of monuments around the world which could be considered archaeological celebrities: sites such as Stonehenge, Machu Picchu, the Great Pyramids of Giza, for instance. Monuments of that order were not only of immense importance in the past, but continue to resonate in the present, and presumably will into the future too; they seem to insist on holding a place in our consciousness.

Professor Colin Renfrew once noted that Newgrange is "unhesitatingly regarded … as the great national monument of Ireland".[1] Newgrange takes pride of place in documentaries about Ireland, in countless academic and popular books, national tourism campaigns, and so on. Yet even though fêted in the media and in academic works, somewhat surprisingly, there is something of an absence when it comes to knowledge of its origins. One might be forgiven for concluding that Newgrange and its sister sites Knowth and Dowth arrived fully formed, out of the blue. In most accounts, when the question of its origins are broached, similar tombs in mainland Europe, especially older passage tombs in Brittany and Iberia, are referenced. Yet, as discussed below, continental passage tombs cannot quite account for the unique expression of passage tomb construction and ritual found in Ireland and at Newgrange.

A close examination of the passage tombs of Ireland, however, reveals that the *je ne sais quoi* of Newgrange may in fact lie hidden in plain sight. Across this island, one can observe increases in the scale and sophistication of passage tomb construction, developments in the styles of megalithic art, advancements in the scale and craftsmanship of the artefacts associated with the monuments, *etc.*, which, taken together, indicate a lengthy process of development. In short, there is an untold history at Newgrange – an island-wide story of incremental changes over hundreds of years, of a society in evolution, perhaps *in extremis*, which left behind such an enigmatic, rich and patterned legacy.

In this book, I will present those developments, that unfolding, examining the factors which ultimately gave rise to Newgrange. Yet, unlike the tourist with limited time who hurries into Newgrange soon after parting with their ticket fee, our journey to Newgrange will be more considered. Like the famed river which surrounds the Boyne complex, we will approach the monument slowly, weaving a path from a distance. We begin with recent evidence regarding the earliest known Irish passage tombs. A series of new dates from the monuments at Carrowmore, Co. Sligo and other evidence demonstrate that some passage tombs in Ireland were in use long before Newgrange was built. This new chronological context creates a platform from which we can cast our eyes over the developmental history of passage tombs on this island, and thus begin to piece together the deep history of Newgrange for the first time.

However, the origins of Newgrange are not just about dates and older sites, the kind of discussions beloved by archaeologists, but about what motivated people. Our purpose will not only be to chart the back-history of Newgrange, but to attempt to discern why it was constructed, what was its role. An answer to this question might also be contained in the developmental history of the passage tomb tradition. In the Boyne Valley, through Newgrange, we have evidence not only of extraordinary physical accomplishments but of tremendous acts of imagination, a testament to rich and developed inner worlds. An interest in an otherworld, which could be embodied by and accessed through passage tombs, may have been a central motivator in passage tomb construction from its earliest beginnings. The limited scale of the first passage tombs – simple monuments with chambers of only five or six stones covered with a large boulder – suggests they were primarily constructed for the deposition of human bones (rather than for internal ritual). Their coastal location may hark back to real or mythic places of origin, over the sea, to the world from which genealogical ancestors came, or perhaps to a land of the dead, a mystical otherworld over the horizon.

Later, larger more sophisticated passage tombs were constructed, with carefully constructed lintel-topped passages which led to sizeable inner chambers. These developments allowed engagement with other worlds to go one step further. Through occupying the same space as the bones of their forebears, select individuals could now physically enter the otherworld, the realm of the ancestors. There, they created and interacted with powerful abstract symbols carved into stone. The individuals who entered the darkened chamber may have been imagined as having been transformed by the experience. At some monuments, at significant points in the solar calendar, they shared the internal space with beams of sunlight. They were introduced to spiritual powers, and perhaps trained in ritual and spiritual techniques. Here it is proposed that this otherworld religion, centred on emotionally intense events experienced by individuals who spent time in passage tomb chambers, was at the very heart of the passage tomb tradition in Ireland.

In the final part of this book we see how, over time, this religious movement which had been growing and changing over the Neolithic began to take a central place in society. It is from this tradition that Newgrange and similarly ambitious monuments eventually arose. That most spectacular flowering of passage tomb construction saw the erection of a small number of massive structures with a peculiarly public focus, together with a distinct change in the role of the monuments. At Newgrange, celebrations connected to the return of the sun at the winter solstice may have been mirrored in the outer landscape by the return of spawning salmon to the Boyne River and other potent indicators of the revitalisation of the natural world. Concerns about the harvest, worsening climate, the need to construct ever greater monuments to venerate the ancestors, and the ability of spiritual and political leaders to negotiate with otherworld powers may have become crucial at this time.

This otherworld-focused religion became central to Boyne Valley communities, transcending its creators, arguably surpassing and outliving their many other achievements. It is extraordinary that this population could invest so much energy and imagination into their creative vision. By the end of the fourth millennium BC, so much of this society's efforts were being poured into ever greater monuments that, between the gathering of materials from the wider landscape, construction, and ceremony, these sites must have consumed much of peoples' day-to-day lives. It is this religion of the monuments, the journey to Newgrange, which is considered in this book.

Newgrange before Newgrange

Rome was not built in a day, and neither was Newgrange; it is the product of accumulated experience gained through the construction of many similar monuments over a considerable time-frame. Even if one were to look at the evidence from the site in isolation, it would be apparent that these communities drew on great experience in its construction. M. J. O'Kelly and his fellow excavators were particularly impressed when they discovered that the builders had cut deep grooves into the roofstones at Newgrange to channel rain-water away from the chamber (Fig. 0.1; Plate 8, lower), and made putty from burnt soil and sea-sand to use at interstices in the passage roof to further ensure the structure's water-tightness, thus solving what may have been a long-standing problem with this type of architecture.[2] These were not *post hoc* additions to the monument, but knowledgeable responses to recognised strengths and weaknesses of these buildings, conceived by communities with great experience of passage tomb construction. Where could this detailed knowledge and experience have come from?

A partial answer to this question is found hidden within Newgrange. Various strands of evidence indicate that some stones at Newgrange (and Knowth) were drawn from older structures and recycled for these 'new' monuments (See Chapter Seven).[3] In some cases, stones with older styles of art were intentionally turned away from the viewer's gaze, deliberately hidden from view. Alternatively, designs were carefully erased using a technique known as pick-dressing,

Figure 0.1. Grooves cut into the upper faces of roofstones to channel water away from the structure (after O'Kelly 1982, fig. 18b).

which removed the layer of stone on which the art was carved. It appears that attempts were made to disguise this more ancient history. Through excavation and recording, however, it is becoming apparent that Newgrange houses within itself a more ancient history.

Perhaps even more dramatically, it would appear older, more obscure 'Newgranges' once stood on the current site. Evidence of earlier monuments, or earlier versions of the current monument, can be found deep within its cairn. Of particular interest is an unusual turf mound discovered inside the tumulus during excavations, potentially covering an earlier monument. Additionally, aspects of the monument's design and the apparent reuse of some materials in its construction indicate potential phases of reconstruction. In short, it seems that Newgrange had several incarnations. And it carries within it the marks of those former lives. It is not only one of the greatest works of the Neolithic communities in Ireland, it actually houses some of that history within itself in the form of earlier structures, materials from more ancient sites, older styles of art, and so on. In an odd way, Newgrange is a museum of itself.

So where should we look to discover the origins of Newgrange? Where could this refined knowledge of construction have sprung from? How and where did the belief systems represented by the monuments in the Brú na Bóinne passage tomb complex develop? Where did the unique canon of artistic motifs originate, as well as the preoccupation with the sun? In short, where can the monuments on which Newgrange was based be found, the sites which represent the inevitable trial and error leading up to its construction? Those who have looked into this question have traditionally turned to continental Europe for answers.

International relations

Newgrange is unique. But it is certainly not an orphan. It is part of an extended family of monuments spread over much of western Europe, from Sweden to southern Portugal, and even as far east as central Poland. Some of the passage tombs in other regions, especially on the Continent, are significantly older than the Irish examples. Consequently, when the origins of Newgrange have been sought – quite reasonably – those monuments have been turned to for answers, especially to Brittany in France where some of the oldest passage tombs in Europe are located, some a thousand years older than Newgrange.

The French/Breton colonisation hypothesis reached a high-point when cultural historical archaeology was at its peak, into the 1970s in an Irish context (though arguably lingering until the early 1980s). Archaeologists then considered Newgrange one of the earliest Irish passage tombs, built by colonists who had journeyed by boat from north-west France and up the Boyne River, and smaller less sophisticated passage tombs, such as those at the Carrowmore complex, Co. Sligo, as later constructions.[4] A variation on this model, but with an opposite developmental sequence, was proposed by Frances Lynch in the late 1970s and again by Alison Sheridan in the mid-1980s.[5] Sheridan in particular promoted north-west France as providing the impetus for the passage tomb construction in Ireland (and Britain), but with the simple passage tombs at Carrowmore and similar sites in the north-east of the island providing the evidence for the earliest wave of megalithic construction in Ireland. She proposed that a construction sequence of Irish passage tombs can be discerned from the simple monuments at Carrowmore, to ever greater passage tombs, and eventually to super-sites such as Newgrange.

The French transmission theory has much in its favour. The passage tombs there are certainly older than those in Ireland. Agriculture was practised in France before it took hold in Britain or Ireland (and, in general terms, the developments associated with the Neolithic came from the east). Brittany is the closest part of mainland Europe to Ireland – the shortest route from northern Spain is almost twice as great. With respect to specific comparisons, many of the design features at Irish passage tombs are found in France, such as corbelled roofs and subdivided chambers, for instance. Additionally, some of the French sites have megalithic art similar to that found on Irish passage tombs, most notably perhaps Gavrinis in Brittany.

However, the Gallic hypothesis has weaknesses, too. In a number of ways, the traditions found in Ireland differ from those of France (and other passage tomb regions). As Muiris O'Sullivan has noted, the Irish monuments stand 'slightly aloof' from their European counterparts.[6] Notably, different funerary rituals are associated with the Irish and French sites. Cremation is most typical at Irish passage tombs, whereas in France, unburnt human bone more commonly occurs. This has considerable bearing on the question of how related these sites may or may not be; divergent funerary rituals may even be an indication of different religious beliefs in either region.

The morphology and design features of passage tombs can vary considerably too. An emphasis on circularity is a feature of almost all Irish passage tombs, but is not as pronounced in other regions. For instance, many of the Breton and Orcadian monuments are encased in long rectangular or sub-rectangular mounds. Stone kerbing along the perimeter of cairns is a typical feature at the Irish sites, unlike most other European passage tomb regions. Though corbelled roofs are a feature of passage tombs in Ireland, the Orkney Islands, and Brittany, they are constructed differently in each area. This, as Chris Scarre has observed, indicates that knowledge of corbelling was widespread, but local communities reacted and implemented the technique after their own fashion.[7] The monument's internal construction can differ also. Newgrange is famous for its three-recess design. A subdivided chamber is a common feature at Irish passage tombs: three-, five- and even seven-recess chambers are found. By contrast, only around 10%

of Breton passage tombs are subdivided.[8] Once again, this would seem to suggest a different response in Ireland.

Similarly, divergences are apparent with respect to the artefacts associated with the monuments in each region, and how those objects were employed. Pins made from bone and antler, a prominent feature of Irish passage tombs, tend not to be found in passage tombs on the continent (though somewhat similar pins appear in settlement contexts in central Europe).[9] The stone balls which occur in the chambers of the Irish sites are not present in the French monuments. Equally, the stone basins often found in the Irish monuments appear to have developed on this island as there is little evidence for similar basins in France or other passage tombs regions in Europe.[10] These artefacts are testament to the dynamism of Irish passage tomb elaboration and the peculiarities of ritual associated with this island.

Differences are apparent with regard to the carvings found on the construction stones of passage tombs in Ireland and elsewhere as well. Though the art found at the Irish monuments shares some commonalities with art in other regions, it has its own distinctive character.[11] Unlike other areas, Irish passage tomb art appears to be almost completely abstract (or at least less obviously representational). As regards quantity of art, the Irish passage tomb tradition is unrivalled in Europe. Indeed it would seem Irish art influenced other regions, including Wales and perhaps the Orkney Islands.

Several other design elements also appear to have been of greater relevance in Ireland. For instance, the use of quartz seems to have had a greater role than elsewhere. Here it is often found secreted inside the smaller passage tombs, and later, as at Newgrange, used to dramatically decorate the outside of the monument, in a way unparalleled in other passage tomb regions. Notably, the percentage of Irish passage tombs with astronomical orientations seems to indicate a particular interest in that aspect of monument design (See Chapter Four).

Perhaps most significantly with regard to theories of connection between Brittany and Ireland, in the last decade it has become clear that the construction of passage tombs in each region does not chronologically overlap. Construction of Breton passage tombs is likely to have ended by 3900 BC, almost certainly by 3800 BC, and the most recent evidence from Ireland suggests that passage tomb construction had not yet begun on this island by that time.[12] Therefore, it is no longer tenable to argue that the Irish passage tombs were replicating developments in France on an on-going basis, each new continental design mimicked in Ireland after a moderate time-lag, say of a couple of hundred years. Clearly, aspects of the development and design of Irish passage tombs and of the objects found within them were particular to this island.

Therefore, though Irish passage tombs were constructed after many of their continental cousins, and undoubtedly built with an awareness of monuments elsewhere in Europe, a high degree of independence in design and use is also evident, a local way of interpreting this widespread megalithic phenomenon. These region-specific developments are indicative of an internal trajectory of passage tomb construction in Ireland. It was that evolution, I argue, which ultimately laid the foundation for Newgrange. Small groups from France or Britain may have introduced megalithic construction to this island, but the idea was taken forward in a distinct and novel way. These immigrant agriculturists knew the power of a few small seeds. Those first passage tombs spawned a wave of innovative megalithic design and construction that continued for over half a millennium. So successful were the communities that built Irish passage tombs, that construction techniques and design features unique to this region eventually spread to nearby areas, particularly Wales, and perhaps northern Britain as well.

But now, as with a good biography, we must first take a few steps backwards and examine the context from which Newgrange arose. To do this, we must consider a time before our central character took the stage, hundreds of years before winter solstice sunlight first entered Newgrange. In the following chapter, Irish passage tombs and the four major complexes are briefly introduced, but the primary focus is the earliest known passage tombs on this island, the seaward footholds of a tradition that gave birth to Newgrange. So it is not to Newgrange that we first turn, but to those first small coastal sites.

CHAPTER ONE

The Earliest Irish Passage Tombs

Others made shore in different lands, seeds scattered on the winds. A small group rests beside the gathered boulders – before the stone raising. The lineage of the journey takers would be remembered, their spirits return over the sea.

Irish passage tombs, as noted already, display many differences to their continental counterparts. One of their most unusual features is that they tend to occur in groups. In the past, these were referred to as cemeteries; today usually as complexes. The best known are the Brú na Bóinne complex, where Newgrange is located and the Loughcrew complex in the east of Ireland. In the west, though somewhat less well known, are the Carrowmore and Carrowkeel complexes.

Brú na Bóinne is the setting for the enormous sites Newgrange, Knowth and Dowth, but also for a host of smaller passage tombs (Fig 1.1; Plate 1). The majority of monuments are situated on an island-like area of land measuring approximately five square kilometres. A minimum number of thirty-seven passage tombs are extant, but it is likely the original number was once greater. Several unopened earthen mounds are likely passage tombs, and geophysical survey and other research suggests that remnants of up to forty-five passage tombs could be present.[1] The scale and sophistication of the monuments at Brú na Bóinne and the enormous concentration of megalithic art are among the reasons the area was recognised as one of the most important prehistoric locations in Europe and in 1993 assigned UNESCO World Heritage Site status.

The passage tomb complex at Loughcrew is located approximately 40 km west of Newgrange. The complex contains fifteen definite passage tombs, but as many cairns are unopened the true total may

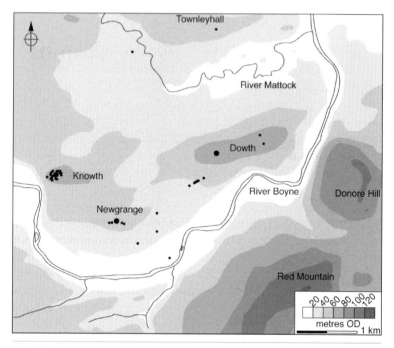

Figure 1.1. Brú na Bóinne passage tombs and related monuments
(after Cooney 2000, fig. 2.3).

be closer to thirty.[2] The majority of the monuments are focused around three main hills. Though not possessing passage tombs of an equivalent scale to the largest examples in the Boyne complex, the complex contains many stunning sites. Cairn T, the focal monument on Carnbane East, is 35 m in diameter and set in a spectacular location, at the highest point in County Meath. It is known for its probable equinoctal solar orientation. One of the more notable features of Loughcrew is the quantities of megalithic art found there.

Carrowkeel is a dramatically situated megalithic complex, primarily in uplands. If unopened cairns and probable passage tombs are included in the total, up to twenty-five passage tomb tradition monuments may be located there.[3] As at Brú na Bóinne, the majority of cairns would fit into an area of roughly five square kilometres. Carrowkeel townland and Keashcorran Mountain are the two main foci. There are also several associated sites on the lower ground however, including the stupendous Heapstown Cairn, one of the largest cairns in the country outside of Brú na Bóinne. The complex is sometimes referred to as 'Carrowkeel-Keashcorran' to highlight the two areas where the most monuments are grouped. In general, the monuments appear less accomplished than those at Loughcrew and Brú na Bóinne, in their current condition at least, and megalithic art is for the most part absent. Yet in terms of its landscape setting Carrowkeel is arguably the most dramatic of the four major complexes.

Carrowmore is of different character than the other three complexes. The passage tombs there are often referred to as dolmens because they are simpler in design and without surrounding cairns. They are usually accounted for by five or six stones, which form a small pear-shaped chamber covered by an unworked glacial erratic. The chambers are further defined through situation on a small artificial platform of soil and stone and a surrounding boulder circle. Most monuments do not have the large covering mounds which are a standard feature at Carrowkeel, Loughcrew and Brú na Bóinne. There are approximately thirty passage tombs at Carrowmore today, though the number may once have been as high as forty five. Older (inflated) estimates of a hundred tombs or more still persist even though there is no substantive evidence to support those claims.[4] In the centre of the complex is a large focal monument with a cairn over 30 m in diameter, Listoghil (Carrowmore 51). The cairn contains a chamber of different appearance than the surrounding satellite sites. The capstone of this atypical passage tomb is decorated with the only examples of passage tomb art in the complex.[5]

Besides these four largest clusters, several other significant groupings are known. Twelve passage tombs are situated at Kilmonaster, Co. Donegal.[6] A significant complex is found along the east coast at Bremore/Gormanstown in north Co. Dublin.[7] Many smaller groupings, sometimes of just three of four monuments are known, for example, at Finner, Co. Donegal or Sheemore, Co. Leitrim.

Other notable passage tombs areas include north-east Antrim and the Wicklow Mountains, though the monuments there tend to be dispersed rather than grouped as at the major complexes.

Passage tomb distribution reflects a preference for the northern half of the island, the majority of monuments located along a band extending from the Boyne River to Sligo Bay (see Fig. 1.2). However, examples have been identified as far south as Co. Cork. The number of existing monuments is not definitive. It can be difficult to be sure about a site's classification if it is badly ruined. Moreover, many stone and earthen tumuli around the country are unexcavated and some probably contain passages tombs. Queen Maeve's tomb and Heapstown, Co. Sligo, for instance, are technically categorised as cairns, even though it is almost certain they are passage tombs. If probable passage tombs are included in the total, then a realistic (and still conservative) number is approximately 260 monuments island-wide.[8]

Though passage tombs exist in various states of repair or disrepair, they display several fundamental design elements which allow us to categorise them, including a megalithic chamber, passage, and almost always a surrounding kerb or boulder circle. Often, the chamber is covered by a cairn and, less frequently, has a corbelled roof, as at Newgrange. Several sites possess passage tomb art, similar to that from Brú na Bóinne. It is these few features, together with the artefacts from within their chambers, which identify them as passage tombs. Yet, several monuments only had some of these architectural features – even when newly constructed – and some can look startlingly different from each other.

The arrow of time

When comparing sites within the passage tomb tradition it is perhaps the sheer variability in dimensions and effort of construction that is most arresting. Newgrange, for instance, is reputedly composed of 200,000 tonnes of material and is 85 m at its widest point. By contrast, Carrowmore 3 is only 13 m in diameter and has a chamber and circle

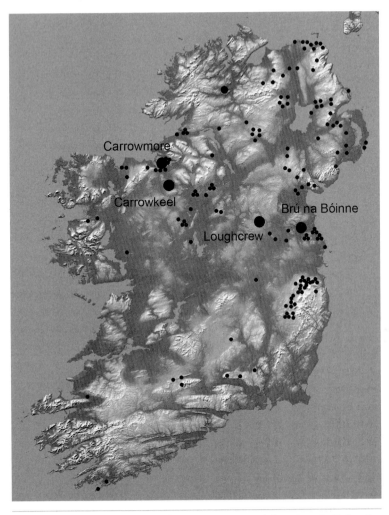

*Figure 1.2. Schematic map of main passage tomb locations in Ireland
(map by Dag Hammar after Eogan 1986, fig. 41).*

composed of just thirty-four stones, many of which are small enough
to be lifted by a single individual. As Irish passage tombs can vary

so much in their scale and morphology, over time, scholars believed that a process of evolution or devolution in monument construction occurred, and that careful analysis would reveal that sequence of development.

Yet, until the nineteenth century, the monuments in the east and west had not been considered connected. One of the first people to make the association was Eugene Conwell, a retired schools inspector, who recognised links between the passage tombs he had investigated at Loughcrew and those at Brú na Bóinne. Not only did he correctly conclude that these two complexes were part of the same tradition, he further proposed that they were part of a chain of monuments extending westwards: "I have little doubt that the cairns on the Loughcrew Hills are but a portion of a chain of such remains, terminated on the east by the great mounds of Knowth, New Grange, and Dowth; and that a fuller and more careful examination of the country will prove that chain to have extended westward to the Atlantic", thus implying the inclusion of Carrowmore and Carrowkeel.[9]

Various surveys and maps of Carrowmore also played a significant role in bringing this most westerly cluster of passage tombs into focus, followed in 1887 by excavations at twenty-two monuments by Col. William Wood-Martin.[10] The artefacts he found removed any doubt that the monuments were a near relation of those in the Loughcrew and Brú na Bóinne complexes. His discoveries consolidated the idea that Irish passage tombs are found from coast to coast. Then, in 1911, R. A. S. Macalister further filled-in the picture by carrying out excavations at the Carrowkeel passage tomb complex 22 km to the south of Carrowmore.[11] This work revealed that the chambered cairns there were also of the same tradition as Newgrange. The discovery meant that similar quantities of passage tombs existed in the west of Ireland (Carrowmore and Carrowkeel) and the east (Loughcrew and Brú na Bóinne).

But the question of which came first, the developed monuments in the east, like Newgrange, or the more rudimentary examples in the west, still remained unanswered. Had there been a gradual evolution from west to east? Or were the sophisticated construction techniques from the east poorly replicated by less ambitious or less resourced groups in the west? Wood-Martin was one of the first to weigh in on the subject, confidently proposing that the large monuments in the Brú na Bóinne complex had developed from the simpler sites: "Between the lowly cists, composed of four or more flags and a covering stone, and the gigantic tumuli of Newgrange and Dowth, there is seemingly a great difference; but that these latter are but developments from the former; through such connecting links as varieties of cromleac-like monuments afford, there can be but little question".[12]

Wood-Martin's simple-to-complex sequential model was soon to be decisively overturned, however. A powerful new explanatory mechanism in archaeology, the cultural historical perspective which developed in the first half of the twentieth century, seemed a perfect tool to explain the sequence of passage tomb construction in Ireland. The large sophisticated tombs at Brú na Bóinne were evidence of the landing point of colonists whose culture and building traditions then moved westwards through a process of diffusion. Smaller passage tombs of less complex design, such as at Carrowmore, were thought to be late in the developmental sequence. As they were geographically removed from the centre of innovation, they were necessarily less sophisticated, and their construction techniques poorer.[13] This also explained why the monuments lacked artwork. The difficulty with this model, however, was that there were so few radiocarbon dates from passage tombs outside of Brú na Bóinne that the east-west diffusion model was purely theoretical.

Cultural historical thinking was soon to receive a fatal blow, however. As radiocarbon dating became more common in the 1960s and 70s, cultural historical models began to collapse; indeed, in some instances the new dates supported a reversed chronological sequence. It appeared invasion and diffusion were not the only way change could happen in a society. In some cases, the appearance of new artefacts, burial traditions, or monuments could be the result of a process of internal evolution, a society passing through various stages from mobile hunter-gatherer groups to segmentary society to chiefdom.

Alternatively, an indigenous group could, of their own volition, adopt an idea such as megalith building from elsewhere, thus opening up the possibility of independent centres of innovation.¹⁴ In Ireland, this new archaeology gained support through a pivotal series of excavations at the Carrowmore passage tombs. Work began there in 1977, just two years after the excavation and reconstruction at Newgrange was completed by Professor M. J. O'Kelly (1962–75). The Carrowmore excavations proved crucial not only to models of the chronology and sequence of Irish passage tomb construction but, as we will see, to understanding of the history of Newgrange.

Carrowmore re-visited

The excavations led by Göran Burenhult at the Carrowmore passage tombs from 1977–1982 and 1994–1998 had the stated aim of clarifying the construction, use, and date of the most westerly passage tomb complex in Ireland.¹⁵ Shortly into the first excavation campaign, several of the excavated charcoal samples returned surprisingly early dates. Some were so early that they led the excavation director to conclude the monuments' construction must have taken place before the arrival of farming to Ireland.¹⁶ Was Carrowmore an independent centre of invention, perhaps the work of 'complex' hunter-gatherers? In the new somewhat revolutionary climate following the demise of cultural historical archaeology it seemed almost anything was possible; older ideas were being abandoned at pace.

An outcome of the Carrowmore excavation dates was that the east-west developmental sequence of passage tomb construction came to be abandoned. Though archaeologists disagreed about the implications of the dates, and serious objections were forthcoming with respect to the Mesolithic builders interpretation, it was apparent that the smallest and simplest sites tended to be early in the sequence of Irish passage tomb construction.¹⁷ But many questions remained. Could hunter-gatherers really have constructed megalithic tombs? If not the work of indigenous hunter-gatherers, could some of the dates provide evidence for a particularly early arrival of colonists before 4000 BC, Ireland's first farmers? It seemed that even after the excavation of eight monuments over a twenty-year period, there were still no answers, no objective or reliable chronology for the construction or use of the Carrowmore passage tombs. A new project was required to re-date the activities at the monuments. In 2005 *The Carrowmore Pins Project* attempted to address this problem.[18] This project sought to examine the use of the monuments rather than seek 'construction dates'.

A recurring feature of passage tomb assemblages is a distinctive form of pin usually made from animal bone or the antlers of red deer (Fig. 1.3). Helpfully, such pins are a core passage tomb artefact and therefore likely to be associated with the Neolithic use of the monuments. Twenty-five samples were selected from two monuments, Carrowmore 3 and Carrowmore 55A. Carrowmore 3 had previously produced two of the earliest and most contested charcoal dates from the two excavation campaigns and therefore had a pivotal role in sustaining the Mesolithic megaliths chronological interpretation. The new dates, when modelled using Bayesian statistical techniques, indicated the most likely start date / age of pins to be between 3775–3520 BC.[19] These dates confirmed that the Carrowmore monuments were Neolithic rather than built by Mesolithic groups, much younger than proposed previously. Nevertheless, they provided solid evidence for some of the earliest use of passage tombs in Ireland.

This interpretation is supported by palaeontological data from two lakes near Carrowmore, Cooney Lough, six kilometres to the west of the complex and Lough Dargan, six kilometres to the south, which demonstrated that agriculture is unlikely to have begun in those areas until after 3750 BC.[20] The dates mirror large-scale studies at a national level in the last ten years which demonstrate little evidence for full-fledged agriculture in Ireland before the second quarter of the fourth millennium BC.[21]

The Carrowmore monuments were not built by Mesolithic groups and probably not built before 3750 BC and greater clarity had been brought to the chronology of Carrowmore, but what could the new dates tell us about the overall sequence of passage tomb construction;

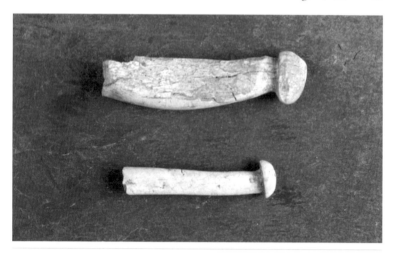

Figure 1.3. Passage tomb pins (photograph © National Museum of Ireland. Photographer Bryan Routledge).

what could it tell us about Newgrange? The new dates confirmed that Carrowmore had to be in use at least several hundred years, perhaps up to five hundred years before Newgrange was constructed. It appeared that the type of passage tomb found at Carrowmore was early in the sequence of passage tomb construction, an ancestor of Newgrange.

These older passage tombs deserve closer examination as they have much to say about changes over time in the Irish passage tomb tradition and about the origins of Newgrange. The excavations of ten of the approximately thirty Carrowmore sites demonstrated some radical differences compared with the larger more typical passage tombs. To begin with, the majority are rather small; they have polygonal chambers and an internal volume of only about one cubic metre (Fig. 1.4). The elaboration of chamber design found at many other passage tombs is largely absent. Objects could be inserted into the chamber but that would have been the limit of their accessibility; most are too small for a person to enter, for instance. They are surrounded by a circle of boulders, often vertically set (unlike most

Figure 1.4. Carrowmore 3 (photograph: Ken Williams).

passage tombs, which typically have horizontally lain kerbstones). The surrounding boulders were designed without spaces between them and hence do not encourage access to the interior.

These sites often have a rudimentary passage. Indeed, it is possible that most of the Carrowmore monuments originally had such a corridor.[22] The passages, however, do not reach the edge of the circle. This is significant, as at other passage tombs the passage typically extends as far as the extreme edge of the cairn, thus allowing someone to pass inside the monument from the edge of the circle. The design of the simple passage tomb appears to discourage entry.

Many of the Carrowmore tombs may never have had substantial covering cairns.[23] Until the excavations, it would have been assumed that cairns had once surrounded the central features but that they had been robbed-out in the modern era. The excavations revealed, however, that throughout prehistory burials and ritual activities had taken place in the space between the outer circle and the central megalithic feature, *i.e.*, activity which could not have occurred if a large covering cairn had been present.[24] Yet it is likely a small amount of protective material once existed around the central megalithic feature, a low surrounding layer of soil or stone. One imagines something of this order would have been necessary to protect the human remains inside, and perhaps to seal in material considered power-filled or spiritually dangerous.

These simple observations regarding the morphology and potential uses of the Carrowmore sites have substantial implications in terms of the ritual practices that could have taken place. As it was not possible for people to enter the Carrowmore chambers, rituals could not have been performed within them (unlike a larger chambered passage tomb such as Newgrange). No megalithic art is recorded on the construction stones of any of the simple form passage tombs anywhere in Ireland. Equally, there is no evidence of astronomical orientation at any sites of this form. These are conspicuous differences with other passage tombs.

So how are the Carrowmore monuments to be understood given these differences in form; is it even correct to place them in the same broad category as the later chambered cairns such as Newgrange? Were the Carrowmore monuments simply deviant constructions, a western folly, or were there other sites of similar form?

An early wave

Over the past twenty years, palaeoenvironmental studies have provided a considerable amount of information about climate change and concomitant oscillations in farming practices in Neolithic Ireland and Britain. It is only recently, however, that robust efforts have been made towards incorporation of multi-scaled palaeoecological data into archaeological accounts.[25] These studies have noted that an improvement in the climate in Britain and Ireland, vis-à-vis warmer and dryer conditions from 4100 BC was likely a critical factor in the adoption of agriculture.[26]

The first substantial evidence for cereal cultivation and house construction in Ireland occurs from 3750 BC.[27] The phrase 'Neolithic revolution' has been out of favour for some time, but the wave of house building and the quantity and variety of archaeological monuments built from 3750–3600 BC perhaps deserves to be considered a revolution, no less so than the industrial revolution of the eighteenth and nineteenth centuries, or the technological revolution of today. The warmer weather and decline of the elm tree (primarily due to disease), provided ideal conditions for incoming farmers. Recent analyses have confirmed that farmers across Ireland were engaged in small-scale fixed plot or settled agriculture (*i.e.* not shifting cultivation as previously thought), which involved intensive effort, tree clearance, building dwellings and walls, and perhaps manuring of fields.[28] This type of life bound people to particular locations and to specific pieces of land.

It is likely that most of the simple form passage tombs found at Carrowmore were built in this period. But passage tombs of simple form with a surrounding boulder circle are not unique to Carrowmore; similar sites are distributed around the coast in the north-west and north-east of Ireland. For convenience, this type of passage tomb will be referred to as Type 1 sites (the first part in a three-fold categorisation of passage tomb considered in this book). Of the north-western group, the monuments at Carrowmore are the best known. There, twenty-four sites are sufficiently intact to assign them to this category. Four Type 1 sites, though badly disfigured, are found above Carrowmore on Knocknarea surrounding the famous Queen Maeve's tomb. Similar passage tombs located nearby, though again badly disturbed, include Abbeyquarter and Barnabrack, Co. Sligo. It may be significant that these latter two monuments are placed at important points of passage through the landscape, perhaps marking territory or routes through the landscape.[29]

Beyond the immediate environs of the Cúil Irra peninsula, further west, several monuments are, or once were, of Type 1 form. A boulder circle at Farranharpy, Co. Sligo approximately fifteen kilometres west of Carrowmore may once have been of similar form, though now missing its central megalithic structure. Two sites at Enniscrone, Co. Sligo *c.* 40 km west of Cúil Irra, though in poor condition, appear to be of the Carrowmore type, replete with boulder circles. Another example,

Figure 1.5. Ballintoy passage tomb (photograph: author).

probably related, is at Carrowreagh, Co. Mayo.[30] The monument, though now heavily overgrown, has a large boulder circle and the remains of a megalithic chamber. In 1779 Gabriel Beranger recorded the most westerly located monument of this type on the grounds of Westport house, unfortunately during the course of its destruction. His sketch and comments about its structure make it probable that this was a Type 1 passage tomb.[31] Magheracar, Co. Donegal is yet another passage tomb that could fall into this category. Though much destroyed and in danger of collapsing into the sea from its cliff edge perch, it is clear that its chamber was undifferentiated and that it lay within a circle of stones.[32]

The second principal region where Type 1 sites are found is in the north-east of the island, the majority close to the Antrim coast. Within that zone, two small passage tomb clusters are found between White Park Bay and the headland north of Ballyvoy, about 15 km apart, both locations facing out to Rathlin Island. Lemnaghbeg, Clegnagh, Ballintoy (also known as Magheraboy or the Druids Stone), Ballyvoy, Cross, Cloghs, Tullykittagh Upper, two sites at Moyadam, and possibly Ballylumford, Co. Antrim all fall into the Carrowmore rubric (*e.g.* Plate 2). Ballintoy is of particular interest as it overlies a cultural layer containing Carinated Bowl pottery (Fig. 1.5).[33] Assuming monument was built soon after the deposition of this bowl it would indicate relatively early Neolithic activity, a time period close to that represented by the new dates from Carrowmore.

Though too destroyed for certainty, it should be noted that other potential Carrowmore-type monuments are found in the east and south of Ireland. Crockaundreenagh, one of a group of three passage tombs at Slievethoul, Co. Dublin, has been compared to a Carrowmore monument.[34] Of two destroyed Co. Dublin sites, Dalkey Commons and Killiney, at least the first may have been a Type 1 site.[35] Equally, though quite disturbed, on the southern coast of Ireland a megalithic structure on Ringarogy Island in the Baltimore estuary, Co. Cork, may also belong to this group. Three kerbstones are still in place and several others are extant but displaced. These surround a mound 5.5 m in diameter, which in turn encloses an undifferentiated megalithic chamber.[36]

Significantly, on the west coast of Britain, are several sites which have been suggested to also be similar to those at Carrowmore.[37] Defining terms such as 'simple', 'closed' or 'polygonal chamber' are used to classify this group, but in truth there are as many differences between these sites as commonalities. Francis Lynch, who was one of the first to discuss this group of monuments in detail, once aptly observed that this group are, "linked perhaps by their very simplicity, rather than by any notably specific features".[38] Most have not been excavated. Two that have, on the west coast of Britain, are Achnacreebeag, Argyll, Scotland, and Broadsands in south-west England. Achnacreebeag is a small site with two megalithic chambers.[39] Three pots found within the outer passage tomb, in particular pot 1, may be related to similar examples from Brittany and Normandy.[40] Broadsands passage tomb is also of interest, and has dates indicating construction in the Early Neolithic at approximately 3700 BC or before.[41] In form, however, it is quite different from the Irish examples in that it possessed ten or eleven low orthostats and was originally covered in a substantial kerbed cairn.[42] Additionally, successive inhumations were found there as opposed to cremations which are more typical in Ireland.

Seven simple passage tombs in the south-west of Wales and around Anglesey may be related to those at Ireland; eight if Trefignath on Anglesey, a multi-period site with an Early Neolithic phase, is included.[43] The various remodelling at Trefignath make it difficult to ascertain whether the site could be related to the Irish examples. Carreg Samson, a monument sometimes included in this group may also be connected, but it is far taller and the construction stones larger than any than other examples, and generally its form lends it a different air to the smaller monuments in Ireland. Though Trefignath and Carreg Samson are atypical, many of the Welsh monuments do have simple polygonal chambers and some have short passages like those at the Irish examples. The small megalith at Bodowyr which forms part of the Anglesey group, for instance, bears considerable resemblance to the Irish examples. However, in general they tend to be badly disturbed and unexcavated, which impedes detailed comparison.

The existence of these monuments across the Irish Sea (especially if additional work should prove them to be morphologically and chronologically related to the Irish examples) strengthens the case for the putative Type 1 passage tombs along the Dublin coast mentioned above. Perhaps other monuments of this form once existed along the east coast of Ireland, or even an Irish Sea group of early wave passage tombs. For Lynch and Sheridan, these sites provide evidence for the movement of groups between north-west France, Britain and Ireland in the Early Neolithic, but further excavation would be required to test that hypothesis. Against this interpretation, simple tombs with short passages and boulder circles, the type found at Carrowmore, do not have exact equivalents in north-west France. Moreover, examples of rudimentary passage tombs are not abundant along the southern coast of Ireland, as one would expect if colonists had landed there from France.

Sheridan proposed that groups may have left north-west France spurred on by ideological, social and economic change which occurred in the Moribhan region *c.* 4300/4200 BC.[44] An alternative possibility, assuming groups did sail from France to Britain and Ireland, is that they left their homeland as the passage tomb tradition came to an end there, just after 3800 BC. If their religious traditions had been under challenge, or groups with alternate beliefs had gained power, then an exodus would be unsurprising. This model would certainly be more in keeping with the new dates from Carrowmore and Broadsands and the most recent data on the beginnings of agriculture in Ireland. Dates on calcined bone from Baltinglass Co. Wicklow (*c.* 3800 BC) also point to early passage tomb activity, though the monument has a more sophisticated form than the sites under discussion here.[45]

As should be clear from these brief descriptions, simply constructed sites may have suffered unequal rates of destruction in comparison to more substantial passage tombs. As they are small and likely had less substantial cairns, they were easier to remove from the land for agricultural or other purposes. The tale of the megalith at Westport House is salutary. After the monument had been delved into and the choicest find (a white stone ball) removed by the land owner (Lord Altamont), workers dug holes and the construction stones were buried – the exact location of the site is not known to this day.[46] It is probably safe to assume, therefore, that in comparison with the larger, less pliant, megalithic sites, Type 1 monuments have suffered a disproportionate level of destruction. Approximately forty-five of these monuments remain in Ireland; about 17% of passage tombs on the island.[47] However, given the uneven level of destruction of these more easily removed and typically lowland sites, it is probable that their percentage would once have been greater, perhaps a fifth of all Irish passage tombs.

In summary, there appear to be two primary regions which saw an early wave of passage tombs construction in Ireland, a north-western and a north-eastern zone. (It may be notable that two of the most important geological deposits in Ireland for tool-making are found in those areas: flint in the north-east and chert in the north-west.) If solitary sites are included in this group, passage tombs of Type 1 form may once have been located around the coast from Counties Mayo, to Sligo, Donegal, Antrim, Dublin, and south to Wicklow.

Type 1 passage tombs on the east coast of Ireland may have been mirrored by equivalent sites on the west coast of Britain. As so few are excavated, however, and several display differences of one kind or another to the Irish group, for the present this must remain a moot point. It cannot be dismissed, however, that more Type 1 sites once existed along the east coast of Ireland, perhaps even in or close to Brú na Bóinne, but over time they were removed or consumed by later constructions. Irrespective of where this type of passage tomb originated, it would appear that the communities who built them were highly successful in Ireland, setting in train developments that would lead to the construction of ever more spectacular monuments.

Calling the ancestors from afar

What was the role of these first passage tombs? It has been suggested that at the beginning of the Neolithic in western Europe a change occurred from burial rites (at sites which were not re-opened after the interment) to ancestral rites (focused on chambered monuments which provided repeat access to human remains).[48] Type 1 sites seem to be somewhere in the middle of this spectrum: they may not have been completely sealed, and they could, and did, receive new deposits of bone, but it would have been impossible for people to enter the sites to carry out ancestral rituals inside the monuments. Only later as larger passage tombs were constructed could individuals or groups occupy an inner chamber, as still happens today at Newgrange.

The contrasts which exist between the different forms of passage tomb are highlighted by the terminology associated with them. Some recent accounts have adopted the word 'temple' to describe passage tombs, in particular Newgrange, Knowth and Dowth.[49] That term could never apply to the Type 1 passage tombs: they are simply too small for the type of events one normally associates with temples, *vis-à-vis* the worship of a god or gods within a purpose-built structure. It would appear that other forms of ritual were associated with the Carrowmore sites, activities primarily centred on the placement of small amounts of cremated human bone (together with other objects from the cremation pyre) within the monuments.

Yet it would be incorrect to think of these sites simply as tombs. One of their most intriguing features is that almost all are located in close proximity to the coast or near a river leading out to the sea. A connection to water is observable with larger passage tombs also, but the degree of association with these smaller examples (or lack of examples away from the coast) is very striking.[50] This apparent interest in locating the monuments close to the sea is so strong that it should perhaps be considered an essential aspect of Type 1 passage tombs. Such a locational preference may relate to the settlements of early farmers, but the connection seems so strong it might also provide a window into the beliefs held by the communities that erected these sites, about their origins and affinities, or perhaps where they imagined departed spirits would travel to after death.

Island peoples who trace their origin to a distant region often look to the sea as the place where their way of life originated.[51] Though there is much of which we are uncertain when it comes to the Irish Neolithic, we do know that cereals and cattle were not native to Ireland and had to be brought by boat over the sea. Given the radical changes in material culture seen in Ireland during the Neolithic, an influx of agriculturalists is probable. If so, it would not be unusual if those first passage tombs were connected with beliefs and traditions about the sea.

Almost all peoples around the world have an origin story. These stories take on special importance if the group in question have moved to a new land or perhaps survived great upheaval or hardship. Narratives such as these help the immigrant community to frame difficulties, to remember where they came from, or to adjust to a new reality. The deposition of human bones around the coasts of Ireland and western Britain may hint at similar origin narratives. These stone monuments may also have served a role in anchoring these people to a land, to their new circumstance.

This practice of placing the bones of select individuals into passage tombs continued in the next phase of passage tomb construction too. However, the many developments which take place with regard to the design and construction of these more sophisticated sites make those passage tombs and the rituals associated with them almost unrecognisable from the simple sites so far discussed. Those new developments in passage tomb construction bring us another step closer to Newgrange.

CHAPTER TWO

Constructing New Realities

Forest felled. The earth opened. The gods of the land must be accommodated; misfortune, disease, averted.

The first generations of farmers on this island must have been pleased with the rich soils and favourable climate they encountered. It would not be long, however, until conditions changed. The warmer, dryer 'honeymoon' period from 4100 BC was followed by a significant downturn in climate from 3600 to 3000 BC. Diseases and pests may also have become increasingly problematic in this period.[1] It appears that during the downturn conditions were generally cooler with increased precipitation across Ireland. Farming communities must have been placed under significant pressure by these changes. A curious, and thus far unexplained, aspect of passage tomb construction is that the monuments increase in size and complexity even as the climate was degenerating and agriculture becoming more difficult. Peculiarly, there seems to be a greater investment in passage tomb construction in parallel with the deteriorating conditions.

The downturn may have been one reason for changes in passage tomb design we see at this time. One of the notable features of this stage of passage tomb elaboration is that the monuments became larger with long passages creating the potential for internal ritual and, at a limited number of sites, for solar orientations. It would of course be understandable if an interest in observing or monitoring the sun through the year gained in importance as worrying climatic changes occurred. Whether this was the reason or not, the changes we see in passage tomb design are dramatic, including an increased importance of the cairn, changes in the design the role of the passage, chamber complexity, and the first occurrence of corbelled roofs.

Passage tombs began to be constructed on a significantly larger scale than Type 1 monuments; most with an external diameter of between 15 and 40 m (*e.g.* Plate 3, lower). These, Type 2, passage tombs were often sizeable and complex structures, and required more people to erect than earlier monuments. Trees may have had to be cleared to enable construction and perhaps managed subsequently. Rocks were quarried. Animals may have been required to drag materials. Skilled people were needed to assemble the internal architecture, and many hands to cover the whole edifice in a mound of stones. The stone cairn became a more significant part of the structure in tandem with the increased sophistication of the internal construction. The cairn was usually kerbed by horizontally lain stones, as opposed to the upright boulders sometimes found in the circles of simple-form passage tombs. An essential aspect of Type 2 passage tombs is that they allowed individual or group entry into an enclosed internal space. Access to the chamber was now facilitated by a covered passage, thus creating a tunnel-like experience (Fig. 2.1).

Type 2 monuments are by far the most typical Irish passage tomb, perhaps representing three-quarters of this class of megalithic monument. With such a large group, other subdivisions could, of course, be made, as has been attempted previously.[2] For present purposes, however, it is sufficient to use broad categories.

Curiously, even though Type 2 monuments are the most usual passage tombs, they have not been investigated to nearly the same degree as tombs of the Type 1 or Type 3 (Chapter Six). The simple form monuments in the Carrowmore complex have been thoroughly excavated; several of them on more than one occasion.[3] The largest passage tombs in the country, Newgrange and Knowth, have also been extensively excavated; the size and spectacular nature of those sites almost guaranteeing they would be foci of research. It is as if the first and last chapters of the passage tomb biography have been read, but not the pages between. Yet this group includes the most typical Irish passage tombs. Indeed, the rituals associated with these sites may lie at the heart of the passage tomb tradition in Ireland. This is why they

*Figure 2.1. Covered passage (partially in-filled), Slieve Gullion
(photograph: Ken Williams).*

are so essential to understanding the additional developments which took place at Newgrange.

As this form of passage tomb represents such a high percentage of these sites, their distribution naturally reflects the general passage tomb distribution pattern; that is, they are predominantly found in the northern part of the island with few examples south of a line stretching from Wicklow to Galway. Typical examples include Seefin, Co. Wicklow, Knockmany, Co. Tyrone and Belmore, Co. Fermanagh, as well as many monuments within the Carrowkeel, Loughcrew and Brú na Bóinne complexes. They are often located in isolated landscapes, perched on hilltops overlooking wide expanses of land, or in otherwise inaccessible locations. One of the defining features of this group of passage tombs is a geographical remove from wider society. The Loughcrew complex, for example, was built at the highest point in Co. Meath. Brú na Bóinne is surrounded by the Boyne and Mattock Rivers which, as Frank Mitchell first noted, had the effect of making the location 'island-like'.[4] Similarly, the Kilmonaster group in Co. Donegal is situated between the Finn and Deal rivers. The Carrowkeel complex is certainly 'a place apart', much of it situated in uplands (Figs 2.2 and 8.2).

It would seem that a degree of isolation from the general community was the key requirement at this stage of Irish passage tomb construction, whether this was maintained by physical isolation in the landscape (elevated land, river boundaries) and/or cultural prohibition. Some form of cultural restriction must have played a role in prohibiting access, as the landscape features that separate these main complexes, though notable in the local context, were hardly insurmountable either. For instance, though the landscape around Brú na Bóinne makes it island-like, it would not have been difficult for someone to physically cross the Boyne at its shallower fording points.[5]

Equally, while Loughcrew and Carrowkeel may well have been perceived as places apart within their local landscapes, the hills on which they are located are not physically daunting. If these areas had been recognised as culturally prohibited, however – for instance, if thought of as a land of the dead or spirits – it would have been considered impossible or perhaps dangerous to access outside of key seasonal religious events. The point is not that they were physically inaccessible, but that they were sufficiently defined geographically to allow them to be seen as separate, to convey 'otherness'. The construction of monumental tombs incorporating bones of the dead would have emphasised that otherness.

Radiocarbon dates are too few to be precise about the chronology of Type 2 passage tombs. Dates that can be tied to construction are especially lacking. Given the limited evidence, we can only suggest they are built after 3600 or 3500 BC. Research at the Mound of the Hostages at Tara, Co. Meath has highlighted the challenges involved in achieving accurate chronologies at passage tombs. Even after fastidious work, incorporating over one hundred radiocarbon dates, uncertainty remains over the period the monument was in use. Though we can say it is roughly contemporary with the construction and use of Newgrange and Knowth, whether it was in use for 350 years or 50 years is still unclear.[6] Continuing work at a national level will hopefully allow more detailed statements to be made about the overall chronology of these passage tombs. Though analysis is still ongoing as this is being written, a series of recent dates from several of the Carrowkeel cairns, for instance, looks set to push back the use-date of those monuments to before the developed phase in the Boyne Valley. Dates returned on antler samples are the earliest, and raise the possibility that the monuments were in use in the middle of the fourth millennium BC, three hundred years before Newgrange was constructed.[7] Monuments of Type 2 design continued to be built and used until the end of passage tomb tradition (even after construction of the largest sites such as Newgrange). Fortunately, chronological models for the end to the tradition are more robust, analysis confirming the early third millennium BC, *c*. 2900 BC, as the end point of passage tomb construction.[8]

Designing for ritual

In our journey to retrace the steps that led to Newgrange, two clear – if crude – categories of Irish passage tomb can now be identified. The first, Type 1 monuments with diminutive chambers; the second, Type 2 sites with tunnel-like passages, significant cairns, and chambers sufficiently large to permit individual of group human access.

By and large, at Type 1 sites ritual activities must have taken place *outside* the monument, culminating in the deposition of small amounts of human bone into a diminutive chamber. Those rituals revolved around the deposition of human bone within the chambers and perhaps ideas around genealogy and the sea. In contrast, the design of the more structurally complex Type 2 passage tombs facilitated human presence *within* the chambers, repeat entry, and potentially diverse religious acts inside of the monument. Human bone was placed into these sites, as with Type 1 monuments, but the rituals associated with this second group may have included additional practises and activities which have not received quite as much consideration. The construction of stone cairns over sizeable chambers had the effect of creating an interior world, a venue for an interior experience of the monument. Intriguingly, with the new design came a host of additional features not present at the smaller passage tombs such as megalithic art, solar orientations and significant changes in monument morphology.

A feature of this second phase of passage tomb construction is that the covering cairn increases in importance, as do the (now accessible) internal features it hides and protects. Physically, cairns surround and support the internal architecture. Many different forms of cairns are found: dome-shaped, drum-shaped, flat-topped and so on. There is evidence that several cairns may have originally had a tiered or stepped design, though today most are roughly hemispherical.[9] Often cairns command great presence in their local landscape (Fig. 2.2). When located on mountains or hills, they can stand out on the skyline and command views over vast areas. Large cairns in lower ground, sometimes of considerable size, can almost appear to be natural hills when seen for the first time.

The passage undergoes an important change at Type 2 passage tombs. At Type 1 sites the passage, where present, is usually very short, a path defined by two small parallel lines of stones. It does not reach the outer circle. At Type 2 sites, this feature transforms into a roofed

Figure 2.2. Cairns G and H, Carrowkeel (photograph: Ken Williams).

tunnel. The passage appears to have changed from a feature associated with the journey of the dead, into one which provides access for the living to the abode of the ancestors.

An aspect of the evolution of passage tomb design is that even though notable increases take place in the size of the cairns and in the length of the passages beneath the tumulus, the width of the passage remains similar. The longest known passage in Ireland is the *c.* 40 m Knowth East. Even at Newgrange and the main site at Knowth, two of the largest passage tombs in Europe, the narrowness of the passages allow only one person to pass through at a time. Though the width also has a structural advantage with regard to the load-bearing function of the passage lintels, other features make it clear that passage tombs were not intended to allow easy entry. Often when traversing the passage, one is required to bow, crawl, or climb over obstacles such as sillstones in order to reach the chamber. A further advantage of the narrow entrance is that the monuments can be easily sealed at the perimeter of the cairn to create total darkness inside. As highlighted later in this chapter, these features may have been motivated by changes in the role of passage tombs. Whatever experience or journey may be represented by these passages, it must have involved considerable difficulty and endurance. What was being symbolised, and why was it that these passages were constructed to allow only one person to move along them? It may be that through this design the builders sought to emphasise individual movement and perhaps individual experience.

Increasingly, more complex chamber designs also seem to be an important aspect of this stage of passage tomb elaboration. Though undifferentiated chambers (essentially a conjoining of an elongated passage and an inner chamber) are found in passage tombs of all sizes and ages – for example, at the Knowth West and at Carrowkeel, Cairn H – there is a definite increase in the elaboration of chamber design as passage tombs suitable for human entry were constructed. The classic passage tomb chamber, composed of three recesses surrounding the central chamber area, as found at Newgrange, became more common. Instances of more elaborate chamber plans are found too, for instance the five- (Cairn F, Carrowkeel) or seven-recess design (Cairns I and L at Loughcrew). One of the advantages of multiple-recess design is that it allowed artefacts or individuals to occupy the recesses and yet the central area could be deployed for other purposes.[10] The possibility that people may have occupied the recesses for extended periods in some passage tombs is considered in the next chapter.

Another important aspect of changes that appear with Type 2 construction is that corbelled roofs are constructed. These structures require a cairn, at least on its uppermost part to act as a counter-weight for exposed corbels. Newgrange has a specially constructed boulder cap for this reason. It may be that the intention to achieve this dome-shaped effect was present at an earlier stage, however. It could be noted that the capstones of most of the Carrowmore monuments have a flat underside and a rounded, dome-like, upper-side. Examples of corbelled roofs are found not only at Newgrange, but elsewhere at Brú na Bóinne and in the Loughcrew and Carrowkeel complexes, as well as at a number of solitary monuments (Fig. 2.3). In some instances these roofs have collapsed. For example, the passage tomb on Belmore Mountain, Co. Fermanagh may once have had a corbelled

Figure 2.3. Corbelled roof, Cairn T, Loughcrew (photograph: Ken Williams).

roof.[11] At Cairn L, Loughcrew, a modern concrete casing has been created to replace the original corbelling.

Corbelled roofs are among the most impressive architectural achievements of the peoples that built passage tombs. The intricacy of their construction causes one to wonder could they be more than an effective building technique for covering chambers of ever-increasing size, or whether cosmological ideas may have been associated with them as well. It may be significant that for many peoples, especially those in the northern hemisphere where the movement of the stars appears almost horizontal, the sky is viewed as a dome or an upturned bowl.[12] Whatever the reason for their construction, over time, the corbelled roof becomes an important part of passage tomb elaboration.

Sense and symbol

Besides overt morphological developments like corbelled roofs, more nuanced aspects of design also feature for the first time with Type 2 construction. In recent years, archaeologists have realised that there are subtle aspects to the construction of megalithic monuments, especially colour and sound, and that they can help us to recognise culturally encoded beliefs.[13]

One of the more interesting areas of research has been into the use of colour in megalithic construction. Newgrange is famous for the white quartz and granite in its exterior construction. The remarkable groupings of coloured stones discovered in 'settings' around the entrances at Knowth are another instance of the selective use of coloured materials. Andrew Jones has analysed the use of coloured stone in the Clyde cairns on the Isle of Arran. He has noted an intentional arrangement of white, red and black stones in the design of Carn Ban. In this case, the capstones of the monument are of alternating white and red schists and sandstones. Jones points out that, "the construction of these monuments does not simply follow the principle of least effort; in terms both of engineering and the availability of stone sources, we may observe a balance between these considerations and the aesthetics of colour".[14] Jones links this use of coloured stones to a set of structured aesthetics that reflected beliefs of the monument builders. It may be significant that the use of paint is beginning to be recognised on construction stones at Neolithic sites in the Orkney Islands and across Europe, especially in Spain and Brittany. The colours white, red and black predominate.[15]

Though close consideration of colour is a relatively recent type of archaeological analysis, to some extent it has long been recognised that selective use of colour is a feature of passage tomb construction.[16] Many passage tombs have a strong association with white vein quartz, which is often found within their chambers or externally at the monuments' entrances. At Knockroe, Co. Kilkenny, O'Sullivan has not only discovered a concentration of white quartz around the entrance of the eastern passage tomb, but has highlighted the positioning of an unusual pink sandstone orthostat in the western tomb. This, O'Sullivan maintains, may have been incorporated in the construction because of its symbolic value.[17]

The importance of colour is apparent in the finds from within the monuments, too. The balls often found in passage tombs are usually made from limestone, chalk or clay. Many of these balls now appear darkened after burning, but originally would have been pale in colour. These light or pale coloured materials, especially the chalk, would have echoed the white quartz and the whiteness of the cremated bone. One wonders was the variety of material chosen secondary to its colour, irrespective of the meaning these balls held. Though this interest in colour may have existed from the time the first Irish passage tombs, its use, especially in construction, appears to significantly increase with time.

If coloured materials could be used in a structured way, could this information help us discern specific beliefs in the past? One of the most important anthropological studies to deal with colour is Victor Turner's famous analysis of Ndembu initiation ritual in Africa.[18] Turner noted a tripartite division of black, red and white in Ndembu rituals. He suggested that a cross-cultural association may exist between those colours and bodily products; specifically he associated the colour black with excrement, white with semen and mother's milk, and red with blood. Christopher Tilley, after Turner, has interpreted the placement of amber beads and red ochre with human bones in Swedish passage tombs as symbolic of a commingling of blood, represented by ochre, with the life-giving associations of the colour white in the form of ancestral bones.[19] Jones too has proposed a scheme based on the choice of materials and artefacts associated with the Isle of Arran tombs. He suggests that white was related to barrenness and the hardness of bones, red with fertility, softness and blood or flesh, and black with darkness and death.[20] Differing interpretations emphasise that discovery of any universally applicable scheme is unlikely. Yet little doubt remains that structured use of colour was taken advantage of as passage tombs evolved, and that in some way this is likely to relate to wider associations present in the Neolithic.

Another novel approach to the study of megalithic monuments has been the investigation of sound within their chambers. Sizeable internal chambers and features such as vaulted roofs would have enhanced acoustic effects inside passage tombs. A number of acoustic investigations have centred on chambered monuments. Aaron Watson and David Keating have investigated sound effects at two Scottish passage tombs, Camster Round in Caithness and Maeshowe in the Orkney Islands.[21] They note that sounds produced in these kinds of environments are not absorbed by the walls, but instead are reflected and hence multiplied, and can appear somewhat directionless. When two sound waves of equal frequency collide, they can increase (or negate) the acoustic effect. Equally, sounds interacting with the enclosed chamber can appeared louder. Watson has mooted the possibility that these and other acoustic effects were used by notional shamanic figures associated with passage tombs to disorientate and confuse the senses in connection to ritual. He proposes that the use of sound in this fashion may have been one way to connote the 'otherness' of these places, and notes that, "Sound brings the world to life. It can appear to fill spaces, create atmospheres, and have an intense emotive power".[22]

Acoustic experiments have been undertaken inside Newgrange, and at Cairns I and L at Loughcrew which indicate that these monuments have natural resonance frequencies ranging from 110–112HZ, a frequency band associated with the lower baritone range of the human voice. Further experiments have attempted to demonstrate that human subjects exposed to this band frequency show changes in the patterns of activity in the prefrontal and left temporal cortex, indicative of trance or hypnogogic states, suggesting that men were involved in some form of chanting in these chambers in relation to promoting experiences of altered states of consciousness.[23]

Though these are interesting areas of investigation, fundamental methodological problems with the analysis of sound properties in megalithic chambers still remain. That passage tombs were acoustically rich places may well be largely an incidental aspect of the materials used in their construction and their form. Nevertheless, it is conceivable that the acoustic properties of chambers, though incidental, could have been noticed and harnessed. Certainly, the changes in the design and construction of Type 2 passages would have provided the possibility of artificially controlling and honing sounds in ways not previously possible.

Right-hand symbolism

Many aspects of Newgrange favour the right-hand side. Standing inside the chamber it is apparent that the whole construction is skewed to the right. The vaulted roof lies to the right of the monument's centre line. The right-hand recess is the largest and the most artwork is found there. Even as the sun comes in, it does so a little to the right of the structure. The chambers of Newgrange Sites K and Z also have emphasis on the right-hand, in both cases having additional construction on that side of the passage. Where could this unusual constructional arrangement have originated? Again, if we look towards other passage tombs in Ireland, it becomes clear that this preference for the right-hand was in fact widespread. The increased size of the right recess is especially apparent in cruciform chambers. As well as Newgrange, Knowth Sites 6 and 17, Loughcrew Cairns H, I, L and T; Seefin, Co. Wicklow, Cairns B, M and N in the Carrowkeel complex and Barnasrahy, Site 5 near Carrowmore all display this curious characteristic (Fig. 2.4).[24]

In the northern hemisphere the sun progresses to the right as it traverses the sky, as do the moon and stars, which may explain the prevalence of this belief. For example, in Irish folk tradition, the right-hand side or movement to the right is referred to as '*deiseal*' or 'sun-wise' in recognition that this is the direction of the path of the sun across the sky.[25] A preference for the right-hand can also be noted in the clockwise growth of plants, or right-hand spirals found in many shells and almost all animal horns.[26] If the right-hand was considered preferable because it was indicative of the path of the sun or growth, placing human art or bone and other objects in the right-hand chamber of a passage tomb may have been thought more

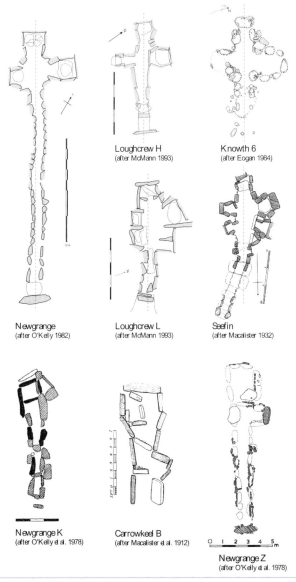

Loughcrew H
(after McMann 1993)

Knowth 6
(after Eogan 1984)

Newgrange
(after O'Kelly 1982)

Loughcrew L
(after McMann 1993)

Seefin
(after Macalister 1932)

Newgrange K
(after O'Kelly et al. 1978)

Carrowkeel B
(after Macalister et al. 1912)

Newgrange Z
(after O'Kelly et al. 1978)

Figure 2.4. A selection of passage tombs with emphasis on the right-hand side (after Robin 2008, figs 7.14 and 7.15).

propitious. Whatever the explanation, this is an example of a concept which became explicitly enshrined in the architecture as Type 2 passage tombs were constructed.

Solar orientations

Newgrange is perhaps most famed for its winter solstice orientation.[27] As with other design features at Newgrange, its astronomical function is not unique; there appears to be a tradition of astronomical orientation in the Irish passage tomb tradition (see Chapter Four). Though archaeoastronomical claims for certain prehistoric monuments were questioned in the past, clear evidence exists that orientating monuments to the sun was of importance to the creators of Irish passage tombs.

Even at a general level, directionality and orientation are central to passage tomb design. Besides alignment towards an astronomical body, many passage tombs are aligned to other objects, often monuments, or prominent landscape features. Equally, examples of monuments whose passages are directed towards a central area or focal site of a monument cluster are relatively common, as at Carrowmore and Knowth.

The existence of a defined and sometimes lengthy passage predisposes these sites to directional forethought. This in itself suggests specific ritual protocols and thoughtfulness. The layout of some passage tombs may have begun in some instances with lines defining the axis of the monuments. Examination of the ground plans of one hundred Danish passage tombs has demonstrated that the laying out of the passage was among the earliest parts of the construction to be erected.[28] Investigations at 'Kong Svend's Høj' passage tomb revealed a row of stones stretching at least 1.5 m beneath the mound to the rear of the back wall of the chamber. The investigators observed that this line was a continuation of the line of one wall of the passage, and suggest that it was a 'sighting line' laid out at the beginning of the monument's construction, previous to the construction of the passage orthostats. A similar pattern was revealed at eighty-six of the one hundred passage tombs examined in Denmark. In each case, the line of one or both of the passage walls appears so harmonious with the chamber that either the innermost part of the passage was constructed at the same time as the chamber, or – more likely – the line of the passage was the first part of the construction established.

Although alignments on a central monument or a distant feature are of interest, it is astronomical orientations that are particularly arresting from the point of view of addressing the Neolithic worldview and beliefs. Of the main megalithic traditions in Ireland, it is only in the passage tomb tradition that a concerted focus on the movements of a celestial body is apparent, especially on important junctures in the solar cycle. It is possible the tradition of astronomical alignment began when Type 2 passage tombs were constructed; the inclusion of solar orientations perhaps connected with a downturn in climate from 3600 BC. If so, an aspect of passage tomb construction which may have had only moderate relevance in the earlier part of the developmental sequence began to take on additional importance in parallel with negative changes in climate. Solar-orientated passage tombs could have provided a certain reassurance to communities concerned about their harvests year-on-year, or allowed them to placate the sun, or a solar deity perceived to be in decline. In Chapter Four we will see that the opportunity to view the sun at close quarters may have raised religious and perhaps even philosophical questions.

Several significant junctures in the solar year are accounted for in Irish passage tomb orientation; at least the winter solstice and the summer solstice, sunrise and sunset, and possibly the equinoxes as well. Only four equinoctial orientations are known from Irish passage tombs indicating it may not have had the same importance as solstitial orientations.[29] This seemingly dedicated study of the solar cycle by Neolithic communities, suggests it was a fundamental feature of the design of some sites, necessitating potentially complicated planning. Again, Type 2 passage tombs seem to explicitly enshrine concepts and beliefs, and perhaps also the concerns of wider society.

Megalithic Art

Megalithic art is commonly found on the construction stones of passage tombs, inside chambers, on the passage orthostats and on kerbstones. It is not associated with Type 1 passage tombs, but only appears as Type 2 sites are constructed, especially in the eastern part of Ireland and western Wales. It is one of the most memorable aspects of design at Newgrange and also one of the most intriguing and mysterious elements of passage tomb construction in general.

Picking is the usual technique for creating the art, using a fine tool with a hard tip (quartz or flint) and a mallet (probably wooden).[30] Once an initial design was picked out, the pitted channels may in some cases have been rubbed with small stones to deepen the design, for instance, at the entrance stone at Newgrange. The Irish art is characterised by designs that include circle, cupmark, spiral, lozenge/triangle, U-motif, zig-zag, serpentiform and radial forms. These core motifs are sometimes combined to make complex and beautiful designs. Designs created using a relief technique are also not infrequent, as found on the lintel of the roof-box above the entrance to Newgrange.

In Ireland, by far the greatest amount of megalithic art is found in the Brú na Bóinne complex, at Newgrange, and especially at Knowth.[31] There are other significant locations for passage tomb art, however. Around one hundred and twenty stones in Loughcrew have art. Work at Knockroe, Co. Kilkenny has revealed approximately thirty stones with megalithic art making it one of the most decorated monuments outside of Brú na Bóinne. At Millin Bay, Co. Down, sixty-four stones bear art, but the monument and the art are somewhat atypical. Another seventeen decorated stones are found at Fourknocks I. Other well-known sites for megalithic art include Sess Kilgreen and Knockmany in Co. Tyrone, and Seefin and Baltinglass Hill in Co. Wicklow. Megalithic art is especially associated with passage tomb complexes; over 80% of the known corpus is found there.[32] Four examples have recently been recorded at Carrowmore and Carrowkeel complexes.[33] Clearly, the creation of megalithic art was a widespread and long-lived tradition.

The precise extent of the corpus of passage tomb art in Ireland is not as clear as one would expect after many years of cataloguing. Older estimates propose a total of approximately four hundred stones in Ireland; two hundred and thirty three in the Boyne Valley and around one hundred and fifty spread around the rest of the country.[34] A subsequent account raised that figure to five hundred and seventy stones, four hundred and eight of which are in the Boyne Valley.[35] The largest total including all potential examples, proposes a total of nine hundred stones countrywide.[36] Though figures have of course changed as a result of excavation and new discoveries, other factors influence the assessment, including the criteria by which carvings should or should not be considered passage tomb art. Some scholars discount the collection of unusual art from the anomalous megalithic structure at Millin Bay. Others would be less inclined to see pick-dressing as 'art' (as it often destroys art). Then there are stray finds of stones with art similar to that found on passage tombs but not associated with a monument. Whichever figure one opts for, it is clearly an enormous amount of art, and illustrates that Ireland was a major hub of artistic innovation in this period.

Many and varied ideas about the meaning of passage tomb art have been proposed since interpretation began over three hundred years ago.[37] In the eighteenth century Charles Vallancey felt confident he could translate the 'symbolic characters' found on the construction stones of passage tombs. In one instance, he translated the carvings on the ceiling stone above the east recess at Newgrange as the 'house of God'; other pieces of art were variously deciphered as 'to the great mother Ops, or the great mother Nature' and 'the sepulchre of the Hero'.[38] Though his methods could at best be described as untempered, his conclusions betray many of the prevailing ideas of the time: the monuments, and hence the art, were linked to sacrifice, the burial of elites, and to a goddess of the earth. In other interpretation, spiral designs have been associated with the eyes of a goddess or various motifs have been thought representations of the sun or the moon. The discovery and validation of astronomical alignments at several passage tombs, especially at Newgrange, has done much to bolster the idea.

A possible weakness with some previous interpretation, however, has been a lack of recognition of the phases of carving. As Andrew Jones has noted, the art has been treated as if it were created in a 'temporal stasis'.[39] Megalithic art is not a homogeneous entity, however; it is a complex aspect of passage tomb design, construction and ritual, and probably had a lengthy history and multiple roles. If the time-depth and stylistic variety within the tradition are incorporated into interpretive frameworks, it becomes clear that there may be several different passage tomb 'arts'. For instance, Elizabeth Shee Twohig who has looked closely into the phasing of the art in Newgrange has proposed three main phases of carvings there, early, main and mature phases.[40] In the passage the earliest phase is represented by art on the back or sides of construction stones, the main phase by a range of typical passage tomb motifs, and the mature phase by pick-dressing, which often occurs over main phase motifs.

Perhaps the most obvious evidence for the layering of different art styles is on stones where 'pick-dressing' is found. Pick-dressing is a technique used to systematically remove the outer layer of stone, the skin, either all over the stone or in particular areas. Sometimes this technique is referred to as 'blanket picking' because all the visible skin of the stone can be removed, which often obliterates previous artistic elements on the stone. It is particularly prevalent in the passage, chamber, and on the kerbstones immediately outside the entrance of Newgrange. An interesting example is stone L19 in the passage at Newgrange, where previous artwork at the base of the stone has been carefully removed and only its ghost imprint can now be seen at its base (Plate 4).

Another example of this layering phenomenon is orthostat 45 in the western tomb at Knowth Site 1 (Fig. 2.5). This stone has been shown to have five layers of superimposition. Two of these layers are forms of pick-dressing ('dispersed area picking' and 'close area picking').[41]

O'Sullivan has perhaps made the most concerted contribution to the identification of artistic styles and phases of passage tomb art.[42] He coined the term 'plastic' art to refer to art with a sculptural quality, as opposed to the more common and simplistic 'depictive' art. This art is fitted to the form of the stone and approaches three-dimensionality.

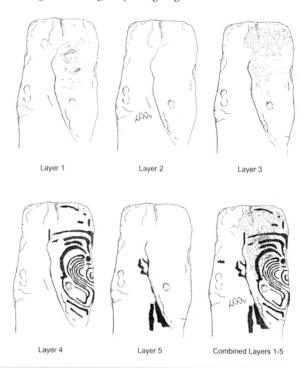

Layer 1   Layer 2   Layer 3

Layer 4   Layer 5   Combined Layers 1-5

Figure 2.5. Orthostat 45, Knowth West (after Eogan 1999, fig. 3).

Plastic art is typically not on the back of stones or on the part of the stone inserted into the ground, which, importantly, suggests that it was completed when the stones were *in situ*. Though the chronology of these stages is not made explicit by O'Sullivan, it is clear that a process of superimposition occurred, previous layers of art overlain to make way for new designs.

Notably, at Type 2 monuments, when carvings are found they are usually within the monument's chamber, unlike at the largest and latest passage tombs such as Newgrange and Knowth where art is also found externally on the kerbstones. At Type 2 passage tombs, the art may have been meant only for certain individuals who were permitted entry into the monuments. In Chapter Seven, the carvings at Brú na Bóinne will be discussed in greater detail as they hold important keys to unlocking a hidden history at Newgrange.

Passage tomb art is one of a diverse set of features which began as Type 2 monuments were constructed. Not only does the first passage tomb art occur in this phase, but the beginnings of solar-orientated monuments, the intentional use of colour in construction and a focus on right-handedness are found too. These features indicate the incorporation of culturally encoded beliefs into the architecture. There seems to be a fault-line in the tradition of passage tomb construction. It is defined by a veritable explosion of new architectural and design features, and, crucially, the possibility for people to go into passage tombs and experience this alternate world. Within these darkened chambers enormous creativity had been unleashed. What was taking place in society and in the environment that could have motivated these dynamic changes?

CHAPTER THREE

Into the Earth

Two days ago they left the village. An offering, our sacrifice. Far away a young man passes through stone; leaves this world. In time new voices will speak for the gods.

So far we have spoken about the monuments in terms of farming; groups that came from abroad and the monuments they built and inspired. However, it must be remembered that during the first centuries of farming on this island, at least two relatively distinct cultural groups were probably present. Almost certainly there were incomers who brought with them not only the necessities for agriculture, but also new forms of houses, developed pottery types, new tools, and, not least, a different worldview. Living alongside those incomers were the hunter-gatherer groups who had occupied the island for at least 4000 years prior to agriculture. Eventually, this latter population adopted farming ways or were culturally subsumed by those around them. This chapter begins with an attempt to understand the experience of those groups. How did they view the changes which were taking place around them? Could their beliefs be accommodated in passage tomb construction?

The incomers had to adjust to a different landscape, climate and soils, but the adjustment for the existing indigenous groups would have been greater. Many changes came with the adoption of agriculture: changes in social structure, in peoples' relation with the animal world, and with regard to how the environment was perceived. Changes in cosmology must also have taken place, in the story about who people were and their relationship to the land. Alterations of this magnitude must have represented a considerable departure for people who previously had a lifestyle based exclusively on gathering, fishing and hunting. Mircea Eliade once referred to this juncture in human history as a 'spiritual crisis', and observed that adjusting to the upheaval of so many values could have taken several hundred years.[1]

As hunter-gatherer society was transforming with the adoption of an agricultural way of life, their beliefs must have been greatly challenged, if not altogether sacrificed. Aspects of peoples' beliefs may have been founded on their relationship to a now destroyed, or at least radically altered, environment. If so, serious cultural crisis could have ensued as the landscape was harnessed and transformed. Altering the earth through farming would necessarily have meant a radical shift in perspective and worldview for indigenous groups. For instance, if parts of the landscape had been held sacred, it would have been controversial to remove or modify its component elements. In particular, the clearance of forestry in the Neolithic would have represented unprecedented change. Equally, if the earth was perceived as sacred, then ploughing may have been considered an offensive act. Such landscape transformations may have seriously challenged traditional belief systems. A case in point is that of 'Smohalla', a nineteenth century Sioux Indian prophet and religious teacher, called upon to engage in agricultural activities:

> You ask me to plough the ground! Shall I take a knife and tear my mother's bosom? Then when I die she will not take me to her bosom to rest. You ask me to dig for stone! Shall I dig under her skin for her bones? Then when I die, I cannot enter her body to be born again. You ask me to cut grass and make hay and sell it, and be rich like white men! But how dare I cut off my mother's hair?[2]

One can appreciate in this statement the rather fundamental difficulties with carrying out agricultural tasks for people accustomed to a different worldview. Even for groups who have long adopted a new way of life, memories of older beliefs may linger. As swathes of forest were cleared, it may have been thought necessary to house the spirits of place, to localise powers that were previously perceived to reside in the landscape. A means of accommodating spiritual entities who were previously thought present in the landscape could have been one strategy to alleviate potential conflict. Passage tombs with increased internal space and fine architecture could have partially resolved the problem by providing a durable place appropriate for the containment of ancestral powers. In this way, as Alasdair Whittle once suggested, megalithic sites may have, "expiated the guilt of beginning to domesticate the natural world".[3]

If these were among the reasons why Type 2 passage tombs were constructed, additional sanctity would have been attached to these subterranean chambers. It would also go some way to explaining the ritual intensity archaeologically evident at these locations. The variety of spiritual practices and activities which formerly took place in the wider landscape had become centralised; the well-being of the group would now flow from there. Perhaps rituals and practices which once took place in the wild (associated with hunter-gatherer spiritual traditions) had become concentrated around passage tombs, places where deities or invisible beings were now thought to reside.

New associations with the landscape must also have been formed. One of the outcomes for people who adopted agriculture for the first time was that they took on a responsibility which was formerly the sole preserve of nature, a co-participatory role in the production of crops and animal breeding. They partook in a direct way in the mysteries of growth, transformation, and decay. How would the land have been perceived by those who engaged in farming? Was it regarded as a separate world, a powerful dimension with the ability to give and perhaps, take life?

The widespread practise of ceremonial subterranean deposition in Ireland and Britain at this time is evidence that Neolithic people perceived the earth to be a powerful and fecund reality. Flint mines, vertical shafts and caves have been found to contain human bones, animal parts, pottery, axeheads and lithics; they were foci for continuous ritual activity. These acts are indicative of a perception of the earth as the source of life, and entrances into the earth as sacred. In the north-west European Neolithic there is abundant evidence that the subterranean plain was imagined as a powerful dimension of reality, a place where life-giving forces resided.[4] It could also have been considered a potentially dangerous alternate world, one which had to be supplicated and appeased with offerings. The construction of a passage tomb could have facilitated control of entry into that realm. For a person to spend time within a chambered monument may thus have been perceived as a dangerous undertaking, as those entering passage tombs were directly accessing the workings of this fertile underground world, the realm of growth and transformation.

The agricultural cycle may have been an important metaphor as agriculture became the predominant subsistence strategy. A seed properly sown and cared for will yield a plant that produces more seeds. These, in turn, can be sown to provide further seeds, so the cycle is unbroken: the death of each plant seemingly begetting its future survival. It would be unsurprising if Neolithic rituals mimicked these seemingly magical processes and cycles: death, a journey into the underworld/subterranean world, transformation, and emergence. Those who went into this realm may, like seeds within the darkened earth, have been undergoing transformative processes. Ideas such as these may have encouraged a belief in reincarnation; were bones placed in passage tombs in the hope that departed persons would be tied to this plain of existence or perhaps drawn back to earth? Reincarnation and rebirth have received almost no attention in studies of the archaeology of prehistoric Europe, even though isuch beliefs were widespread amongst pre-modern peoples. For instance, a substantial study by Antonia Mills and Richard Slobodin of North American native peoples' and Inuit tribes' beliefs regarding reincarnation has demonstrated that most shared beliefs around human and animal rebirth.[5]

Besides the vegetative cycle, other natural cycles also seem to reflect this cyclical perspective. The sun sinks beneath the horizon only to re-emerge the following day renewed. During the year it moves across the sky and back again in a perpetual cycle. The communities that built passage tombs may have imagined the orb of the sun as going down into the earth or the underworld at sunset.

Passage tombs may have allowed access not only to the place from which nature regenerated, but to the place where the sun died and was reborn. An interest in astronomically orientating passage tombs would make sense in this context. Perhaps passage tomb communities imagined a certain symbiosis between these natural cycles and the people who spent time in passage tombs: all going into the earth, the underworld, and later re-emerging transformed and renewed. When people 'disappeared' into passage tombs they could have been considered dead, or in metamorphosis. They may have been absent from the rest of the community for weeks, months, or even years. Later they returned, transformed, their identity and perhaps their role in society re-forged in darkness. Their communities would also have been transformed by the event.

Rites of separation

For indigenous communities adopting the new way of life, the construction of passage tombs which could house spiritual forces may have served to alleviate some of the negative feelings arising from the act of transforming the landscape, and disturbing its spirits. However, it could only have been a partial solution, because communities would still have felt a need to interact with those powers. How could people develop and maintain their long-standing contract with spiritual entities – beings previously believed to be resident in the landscape – in these new circumstances?

It may have become necessary to find new means of engaging with these powers; new practices which allowed certain individuals to engage with spiritual powers inside passage tombs on behalf of their communities. Rituals whereby members of the community were introduced to the guiding powers perceived to reside within passage tombs would have been one way of ensuring that vital relationships between the life-giving forces and the human community would continue to flourish. These individuals would have needed to be freed for a time from farming tasks and wider social requirements.

It is not a new idea to suggest that passage tombs were designed for repeat rituals rather than as simple tombs. However, repeat entry and exit from passage tombs, and chambered tombs generally, has typically been considered only in relation to rituals concerned with the placement of new deposits of bone by ritual specialists. What I wish to propose here, however, is not only that people were re-entering passage tombs for these kinds of rituals, but that at some passage tombs people went in and stayed for prolonged periods inside the monuments, and that this seclusion from the rest of society was connected to ritual training.[6]

The rituals which took place within these passage tombs may have involved various techniques to establish a connection between the individual and invisible beings or the world where these were thought to reside. Extended periods of seclusion in darkness could have had a primary role. The construction of passage tombs with recesses large enough for a person to occupy, where a covered passage could easily block out daylight, would have been ideal to facilitate such an experience.

The cremated and unburnt human bone which surrounded individuals entering the chamber may have enhanced the practices or rituals they were engaged in. Rather than the monuments being houses for the dead and hence becoming associated with the otherworld, it may be that the monuments were seen as the home of otherworldly powers and hence an appropriate place to put human remains. If these chambered monuments were thought of as filled with spirits of the departed dead, only people with a direct association with the otherworld – or those who desired to forge a relationship with otherworldly powers – would have been allowed into the monument. It would probably have been considered foolhardy or spiritually dangerous to enter one of these sites for any other reason. This may have been a trial associated with ritual training, to confront spiritual powers and forces in these darkened chambers. As Guillaume Robin's close analysis of passage tomb morphology and design has shown, the spatial model that guided the construction, decoration and use of these monuments "is very probably the representation of the topography of the other world as it was conceived in Neolithic myth".[7]

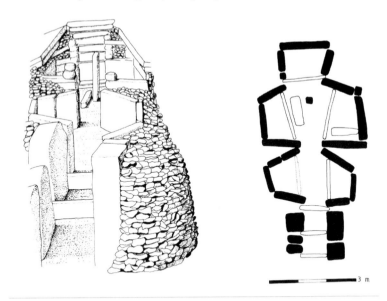

3 m

*Figure 3.1. Cairn F, Carrowkeel, Co. Sligo
(after Macalister et al. 1912, plates XVIII and XIX).*

In passage tombs with undifferentiated chambers only one area could be occupied at the end of the passage, with space for, at most, one or two people. More complex passage tombs, however, had multiple recesses which would have allowed three or more people to occupy the structure. Many, like Newgrange, had a three-recess design, but some had additional side chambers such as at Carrowkeel Cairn F (five recesses) and Cairns I and L at Loughcrew (seven recesses) (Figs 2.4 and 3.1; Plate 3, upper). The ability to accommodate more people inside the monument may have been one of the advantages of larger complex chambers.

If people sat or squatted in side recesses, the central chamber was open for movement or ritual practices. Passage tomb recesses are generally just large enough for single person occupancy (Fig. 3.2). Recesses may have been designed with this in mind, as all can at least accommodate a sitting or squatting adult (perhaps pointing

Figure 3.2. Author inside a passage tomb recess, Cairn G, Carrowkeel (photograph: L. Hensey).

to their intended use). It is interesting to observe that passage tomb recesses appear to remain relatively uniform in size even though the monuments themselves can increase dramatically in dimensions.

Entering a passage tomb effectively separated the entrants from the outside world. All kinds of contrasts were automatically established. Not only was there the contrast between the separated individuals inside the chamber and their families and the wider community outside, but also between the darkness within and the daylight outside, between interiority and exteriority. Inside the monument, sounds may have been experienced differently: those outside muffled or muted, those inside amplified or echoed. Larger passage tombs allowed those within to have particular experiences and engage in specific rituals that could only be experienced because of those design modifications.

If some passage tombs were used for rituals concerned with

retreat and seclusion, what did people experience there? In a variety of religious traditions around the world and through time, spiritual aspirants have engaged in ritual separation from the wider community. For the Kogi, a Tairona people from the Sierra Nevada de Santa Maria in Columbia, seclusion is the primary educational and religious ritual.[8] Someone in training to become a ritual specialist spends nine years, ideally from infancy, in seclusion in total darkness away from the main community. Time spent in ritual seclusion was the primary prerequisite to divinise and make important decisions for their communities. For the Orokaiva of northern Papua, the main period of seclusion for neophytes lasts for between three and seven years, during which time novices must not be seen or heard beyond their place of confinement on pain of death.[9] Though Neolithic people may not have spent these extraordinarily lengthy periods inside Irish passage tombs, we should be open to the possibility of prolonged stays, for months or perhaps even years.

For willing retreatants, darkness in isolation may have been a unique spiritual opportunity. In darkness, memory is encouraged, as less outside influences and interactions are experienced and fewer new memories created. Darkness provides the space to assimilate previous experience. Ideas around gestation may have been relevant. Solitary isolation in darkness would have been difficult. For some participants, the experience may have been mentally and physically taxing, even if it allowed them to develop qualities. One result which could have been associated with the experiences of those who spent time in passage tombs was increased artistic sensibilities. Is it possible that the dynamism of passage tomb art could be partly explained by rituals such as this; the shapes and forms of passage tomb art emerging from the sensation-starved minds of people spending extended periods in darkness?

Art and altered consciousness

It is difficult to imagine what it would have been like for a Neolithic person to approach a passage tomb for the first time, particularly for someone who had been chosen to enter the monument. The journey across the landscape, viewing the monument for the first time and finally entering it, could have been both a terrifying and exhilarating experience. If they believed they would encounter ancestors or their deities, the experience would have been heightened even further. Megalithic art would have had an especially important role in the experience of place, especially the art found deep within passage tomb chambers. This is one reason it has had a prominent place in discussions of religious activities at passage tombs.

From the late 1980s onward, rock art expert David Lewis-Williams and others began to propose that passage tomb art could be derived from shapes and designs observed in trance experiences.[10] According to Lewis-Williams, clinical experimentation on western participants demonstrates that certain images, referred to as entoptic phenomena, are hardwired into the human brain. These images are experienced by people in trance states, and can be induced by a range of techniques and practices including sensory deprivation, fasting and controlled breathing. Recorded entoptic forms include grids or lattices, sets of parallel lines, bright dot/flecks, zig-zag lines, nested catenary curves, filigrees and spiral forms, which appear to conform well to the corpus of passage tomb art.[11]

An objection to the trance art model is that it would have been impossible for people in entranced states to actually execute these carvings. O'Sullivan, for example, though accepting a link between passage-tomb art and subjective visual phenomena noted that a critical issue, "the relationship between short-term visual experiences, perhaps in a ceremonial context; and the creation of motifs on stone which is a time-consuming, slow and mundane task requiring the sober and steady co-ordination of hand and eye".[12] Against this, it could be pointed out that the creation of carvings may have taken place in several discrete stages, perhaps initially with only light incisions on stone. This stage of the process could have been achieved by someone in a trance state without much difficulty. Equally, images seen in trance could first have been created in other formats and only later transferred to stone. For instance, sketched carvings may have been executed in wood or bone, though these may not have survived in the archaeological record. Of interest is a small piece of slate found in the eastern chamber at Knowth with a thinly scratched chevron design.[13] Sometime later, when the immediate effects of altered perception had subsided, the scratched motifs could then have been further defined by the various picking and rubbing techniques required for deeper engravings.

As noted previously, multiple phases of artistic creation can be observed in some passage tombs. The art could therefore be reflective of a living practice: the potent environment within the chamber and the previous art which confronted people there motivating people to add new carvings, or rework older ones. At Knowth, the modern observer's desire for completion and final presentation is continually frustrated. Everywhere, images in all stages of completion are found: composed pieces carved to perfection beside designs apparently incomplete or abandoned. The thinly incised designs often found at Knowth in particular seem to indicate that art was created in discrete stages during the use period of the monument (Fig. 3.3). They may represent the initial stages of an artwork, the sketch, or even be the hasty recording of an inner experience or vision prior to later embellishment. Sometimes these incised designs may have acted as guidelines for subsequent angular picking, or perhaps as guides for painted designs.

Nevertheless, most of the visible art at Newgrange is unlikely to have been a direct product of images seen in altered states. As discussed later, art which is most likely of that type – *i.e.*, subjective recording of internal imagery – has been erased or actively hidden at Newgrange. Significantly, of the corpus of art at Newgrange, the more likely examples of recordings of entoptic images were hidden or have been erased. In Chapter Seven, the reasons why this may have occurred are explored.

Modes of religiosity

As noted in Chapter One, in some recent works the word 'temple' has been used in connection with passage tombs. Other accounts,

*Figure 3.3. Incised lines and deeper carving, Knowth West
(photograph: Stefan Bergh).*

especially those that focus on passage tomb art, have alluded to associations with shamanistic forms of religion.[14] The term temple simply could not apply to all passage tombs, especially the diminutive passage tombs at Carrowmore and similar monuments that appear early in the tradition. Equally, shamanistic models based on cross-cultural comparison are probably unsuitable when one considers the societal stratification likely to have been present within the communities that built Newgrange (see Chapter Six). The main problem is that a lengthy evolution in passage tomb design and religion is evident and a one-answer-fits-all approach will simply not suffice.

Indeed, it may be inappropriate to apply the term shamanism to activities of any particular stage of passage tomb construction. Even in Siberia where the term 'shaman' comes from – and some would argue the only place the term should be used – it has been inappropriately applied to a wide range of different ritual specialists who operated there.[15] Similarly with respect to Mongolian ritual specialists, in just one village six distinct types of ritual practitioners could be present. The *Yadgan* drummed, sang, and danced to invoke a spirit they had learned to control, to work with them against other harmful spirits. The *Bagchi,* or male elder, propitiated clan and landscape spirits on behalf of the community. The *Oishi* were female curers working through a goddess-like spirit to assist women with conception and child health. The *Bariyachi* were midwives directly involved in childbirth. The *Barishi* were 'bone-setters'. Lastly, the *Kianchi* represented malevolent animal spirits trying to become human.[16] By current archaeological standards, these various specialist roles could be foisted into the category of 'shamanism'. The term is additionally problematic because of its association with various western shamanic practitioners who represent something quite different than the shamanism of Siberia or related practitioners in other traditional societies.[17] Accepting these reservations, what was happening at this stage of the passage tomb tradition may yet have involved some features shared with what are traditionally seen as shamanic forms of religion, including the separation of the novice from the wider community; isolation in a purpose built structure; emotionally intense rituals; the symbolic death of the novice; and training by elders in religious precepts.

Harvey Whitehouse, an anthropologist with expertise in the cognitive science of religion, has devised a useful paradigm which I think can be successfully applied to developments in the Irish passage tomb tradition.[18] He has proposed that religions have a tendency to deviate towards two core modes of religiosity, or more correctly to two 'attractor positions'. The first category he names *doctrinal.* This form of religiosity involves frequent repetition of religious teaching, and tends towards low level emotionality. Rituals place emphases on steady and continual reinforcement of ideas or beliefs over long periods. A study of seventy-four cultures supported the proposition that, "high-frequency rituals correlate with larger-scale farming societies while more dysphoric rituals prevail in smaller communities".[19] This would make sense as farming requires more communal activities, especially for clearing the ground and harvesting, but also planting, weeding and fencing.

Whitehouse does not see doctrinal religiosity occurring until the development of complex societies. Though interestingly, in recent work with Ian Hodder and others he has suggested that at Çatal Höyük there is evidence for a shift from the imagistic mode to doctrinal religiosity.[20] (In the final chapter the features associated with the beginnings of doctrinal religion are explored further with regard to how they may relate to ritual and ceremony at Newgrange). The second mode of religious transmission, which is considered the more archaic form, he refers to as *imagistic* religiosity.[21] It revolves around high arousal experiences that expose the person to what he refers to as *spontaneous exegetical reflection*; for instance, revelation. Whitehouse describes imagistic modes of religiosity as, "very intense emotionally; they may be rarely performed and highly stimulating (*e.g.*, involving altered states of consciousness or terrible ordeals and tortures)".[22] These emotionally powerful events, which are often difficult or traumatic, can take years or even a life-time to internally process. Whitehouse has borrowed the term *flashbulb memory* from psychology to describe such religious rituals.[23] They are experiences that are so intense or traumatic it is as if a flash has gone off in a darkened room (or in one's mind). An individual might recall all the details of the scene and the associated emotions with great fidelity; the kind of experience that one would remember decades later 'as if it happened yesterday'.

Examples include the traumatic ordeals of Melanesian initiation cults, or widely recorded rituals involving piercing of the skin, burning and tongue bleeding.[24] The short-sharp-shock strategy opens the individual up to an intensely focused state which allows religious ideas to be deeply implanted. With imagistic religion, teachings do not have to be slowly learned and continually reinforced as with doctrinal modes of religiosity; rather the initial emotional event is relatively quick, and then followed by a long period of slow release as the experience is integrated.

Whitehouse notes that imagistic experiences, "tend to trigger a lasting sense of revelation and to produce powerful bonds between small groups of ritual participants".[25] That is, through these intense experiences one can become 'fused' to a group or to an ideology in a particularly strong way.[26] The existence of groups of passage tombs, or of individual passage tombs with multiple recesses, would be fitting in a context where bonding of a group was an aim of the rituals. If ritual training were a short-term event requiring only a few days of isolation from the community, then groups would hardly need the quantity of passage tombs that are found in the major complexes. If ritual training required that individuals were inside monuments for longer periods, however, for weeks or seasons, then creating additional monuments may have become a necessity. The evidence suggests that ritual specialists and novices separated themselves from the wider community within an organised and culturally prescribed group setting.

If the features of the imagistic mode are examined (Table 3.1) they appear to correspond well with the evidence from most Type 2 passage tombs. For a neophyte to be brought to an isolated landscape and then required to pass through an entrance into an underworld, perhaps thought populated by powerful ancestral spirits, would be an incredibly intense proposition, one imagines. Perhaps they experienced

Variable	Doctrinal	Imagistic
Psychological features		
1. Transmissive frequency	High	Low
2. Level of arousal	Low	High
3. Principal memory system	Semantic schemas and implicit scripts	Episodic/flashbulb memory
4. Ritual meaning	Learned/acquired	Internally generated
5. Techniques of revelation	Rhetoric, logical integration, narrative	Iconicity, multivocality and multivalence
Sociopolitical features		
6. Social cohesion	Diffuse	Intense
7. Leadership	Dynamic	Passive/absent
8. Inclusivity/exclusivity	Inclusive	Exclusive
9. Spread	Rapid, efficient	Slow, inefficient
10. Scale	Large scale	Small scale
11. Degree of uniformity	High	Low
12. Structure	Centralised	Noncentralised

Table 3.1. Modes of religiosity contrasted. After Whitehouse (2004a, fig 4.1.)

further physically or psychologically challenging events at the hands of tribal elders. Dwelling in seclusion within the darkened passage tomb chambers over an extended period would have allowed future ritual specialists to process intense experiences or to absorb instructions or ritual knowledge imparted by a mentor or senior ritual specialist.

Notably, the imagistic mode of religiosity is also one that tends to take place in societies without strong central authorities.[27] The revelatory experiences sometimes associated with this type of religiosity are typically thought to come directly from the gods or the ancestors rather than mediated by intermediaries. This style of revelation may go some way to explaining the multiplicity of design features which appear associated with passage tombs, notably the tremendous variability of passage tomb art. Such variation could be a reflection of the diversity of revelatory experiences of those who underwent seclusion.

Yet this multivocality does not appear to last. Society may have become more hierarchical, and authority more centralised as the largest and most complex passage tombs were constructed. At Newgrange, the removal of older art may be an indication that art-making had become something which was more controlled, and perhaps culturally sanctioned (see Chapter Seven).

CHAPTER FOUR

Waiting for the Sun

Within the darkened chamber, they wait, like the bright seeds within the earth. How long before rays of sunlight slowly creep into the passage. In the fields below, people pray for good omens, they pray for the harvest.

Undoubtedly, the most recognised feature of Newgrange is its winter solstice orientation. As with other aspects of passage tomb construction and design, this too can be shown to have developed from previous Irish monuments. Understanding the early history of astronomical orientation is significant not only because it provides important clues to the broader evolution of passage tomb design and ritual, but because it can offer insights into the beliefs and concerns of Neolithic communities. Thanks to Professor O'Kelly's restoration of the passage and roof-box at Newgrange, the winter solstice orientation can still be witnessed (Plate 5), thus providing us with another, more direct, means to explore astronomical orientation. What follows is a first-hand account of the winter solstice experience.

Being there

Over the winter solstice of 2011, I was invited to witness the sun entering Newgrange. *Witness* is a good word, with all its connotations, religious and legal, personal and formal. Being in the chamber for the winter solstice event is akin to being present at a rare encounter between significant cultural or political icons, or perhaps at an emotional reunion between long-separated family members. The meeting in this instance was one of light and place, heavenly and human worlds.

Our group met in the Brú na Bóinne Visitor Centre, crossed the footbridge over the Boyne River, and took the small tourist bus through the fertile Boyne Valley. After a few minutes, we arrived at the lower slopes of the grassy hill on which Newgrange sits. All this happened not in darkness but in the half-light of morning. The sun had already climbed to a little under one degree in altitude as it began to rise over Red Mountain, the hill to the south-east of Newgrange. Only then could it beam its much anticipated light into the chamber. It was surprisingly bright therefore as our group climbed the wooden steps which are the modern means of surmounting the art-covered kerbstones that surround the passage entrance. Outside, hundreds of people were gathered; many who come every year to mark the solstice.

The group passed single file through the passage. The ground rises and the passage narrows as one progresses deeper inside; at a particular juncture one must turn sideways to negotiate inward leaning orthostats. Visitors often tend to slow or stop before this point to do a quick calculation, assess whether they will make it through, or just make sure they are prepared to go the whole way. Reaching the chamber there was barely concealed excitement; the air heavy with expectation. Some of the guests had travelled far, with no guarantee that the sun would appear. Invited groups enter the chamber on the two days either side of December 21, as the solar phenomenon can be equally as effective on those days. Some years the sun has not entered the chamber on any day over the solstice window, and so I was not overly confident. Nevertheless, it had been an extremely frosty night and morning and this augured well for a clear sky.

The master of ceremonies, either the manager or supervisor guide at the Brú na Bóinne Centre, has a difficult duty. She helps keep people relaxed and in good spirits, and yet at the same time has to maintain the solemnity the event evokes. The main task is managing peoples' expectations. If it seems the sun is going to shine in but then fails to, the potential for disappointment is great. The best days are when the sky appears full of clouds and then, just in the last minutes, a clear patch opens on the horizon and allows the sun to burst through into the chamber to surprise and delight. Everything still hung in the balance for our group.

And then it happened. It began with pale ambient sunlight in the passage and chamber. A richer coloured line of light was visible along the edge of this band, like the hem of a dress or the measurements along the edge of a ruler. I had always been a little puzzled by O'Kelly's famous account of the winter solstice sunlight as a 'pencil of light', but then I understood: at first it is literally the width of a pencil.[1] The guide announced to the assembled group that the sunlight was now in the chamber. It reminded me of when the arrival of a president or dignitary is announced before an assembled auditorium. The solstice light had not slowly crept up the passage as participating groups invariably expect, but came through the roof-box above the passage and appeared instantaneously on the floor between the people assembled on each side of the chamber. Even with an intense focus on its arrival, the sun managed to sweep in without us realising. We were immensely lucky; it transpired that this day was the only one of the mornings either side of the solstice in which the beam would enter the chamber. For a brief moment I managed to sink beneath my own expectations, the inevitable grasping after experience, to taste another perspective. I imagined Neolithic people waiting, really waiting, not entering the chamber minutes before the event as we had done, but remaining in the chamber for perhaps hours or days previously.

As the group watched, all intensely focused on minute changes in the light, it seemed we became a single entity; our separate identities temporarily forgotten in the wonder of the moment. The deeper line of sunlight started to increase in width, slowly expanding into the wider band of pale ambient light. But this was no static artificial light; it changed continually; not only with its entry and exit into the monument and its variation in width, but in its tone and colour. Tiny dust particles floated in the sun's light creating the illusion of activity mixed with stillness. It is easy to imagine how the light could have been perceived as animate in the past.

I still see it in my mind's eye, the rich red-gold of the light along the chamber floor. Its height from the floor appeared to me as great as its width, more like a beam of wood in a medieval church's roof than something as intangible as light. Yet this was a permeable beam. Some of the attendees crouched to the floor and inserted their hands into it, as one would in a river, moving them about, bathing them in light. Others placed objects in the light; a wedding ring, a memento of someone recently deceased, a small container of water. For that transcendent moment it seemed the group's day-to-day worldview had been left behind; there was no question of another possibility.

Then slowly, almost as mysteriously as it had entered, the light began to narrow and begin to recede from the chamber. The event was over. Most of the group were smiling broadly, still soaking up the event; some trying to remain in the moment for as long as possible; some already excited to describe everything to friends and loved ones on the outside. Generously, the guide wanted some of the people waiting and shivering in the cold outside to also have a taste of the experience, so our group was ushered out of the chamber. Another surprise awaited. As I moved down-slope through the passage, I stumbled and as I looked up found myself seemingly walking into the orb of the sun; this makes sense of course, as the sun was still directly aligned on the passage (even if not reaching as far into the chamber). For a moment, I was blinded; I could see nothing but intense yellow light completely filling the space surrounding me, as if I were actually entering into the body of the sun. And then out, smiling faces, a little mist on the river, a new morning, the world reborn.

A solar tradition

The winter solstice event at Newgrange is truly unforgettable. Part of the awe engendered in the visitor is that the phenomenon appears so unique. Most people have little sense of the gradual build-up of knowledge of astronomical construction techniques that allowed a monument like Newgrange to be conceived and created. Even in academic circles it took some time before Neolithic astronomical orientations were accepted. Different viewpoints were reflected both by archaeological silence on the issue of astronomical orientation of monuments and a sometimes overly vocal amateur astronomy. This has been somewhat ameliorated in recent years with the increasing development of the discipline of archaeoastronomy, or at least one strain of scientifically stringent and theoretically aware archaeoastronomy.

Astronomical orientation in the passage tomb tradition is accepted based on undisputed alignments at Newgrange and Maeshowe in the Orkney Islands. While most archaeologists agree that Newgrange has a valid solar orientation, there is much less consensus when it comes to whether Newgrange had astronomically aligned precursors. It might almost seem that the astronomical sophistication at Newgrange had come from nowhere; that there were no forerunners, no build-up of information, no less-perfect alignments to represent the inevitable trial-and-error process that must have taken place along the way. Could this be so?

When O'Kelly rediscovered the winter solstice orientation at Newgrange, the monument was considered an extremely rare example of a prehistoric astronomical orientation. However, though less well known than Newgrange, several other sites with solstitial alignments in Ireland and beyond are now confirmed. A comprehensive recent study by Frank Prendergast, based on analysis of 138 Irish passage tombs with passages suitable for astronomical survey, has indicated that twenty-four sites or 17% are orientated on a significant solar declination.[2] Of these, the majority are orientated towards the summer and winter solstices, both rising and setting suns.

Examples at Brú na Bóinne include the south-western passage at Dowth which is considered to have a winter solstice sunset orientation, and the passage tomb at Townleyhall, which possesses a summer solstice alignment.[3] Outside of Brú na Bóinne, a well-known equinoctial sunrise is found at Cairn T, Loughcrew, and two recently discovered solstice orientations at Cairn X1 on Patrickstown Hill, and another at a ruined megalith at Thomastown, southeast of the complex.[4] The two passages of the monument at Knockroe, Co. Kilkenny are believed to be astronomically aligned, one on the rising sun on the winter solstice, the other on setting sun.[5] Another winter solstice sunset orientation is found at Slieve Gullion, Co. Armagh.[6] Astronomical orientation of passage tombs is not restricted to Ireland. In Wales, a summer solstice sunrise alignment was recently rediscovered at Bryn Celli Ddu.[7] Equally, the great passage tomb of La Hougue Bie in Jersey has an equinoctial sunrise orientation.[8]

Most archaeologists are prepared to accept solstitial orientations, but more caution is usual with respect to equinoctial orientations or further subdivisions of the year (such as cross-quarter day or seasonal orientations). There is little evidence of orientation to a major lunar extreme or stellar target (*i.e.*, to one of the brighter stars); not enough to argue intentionality at any rate.[9] Confirming a site's astronomical veracity can be problematic. Even if a monument is apparently aligned on, or close to, a significant event or object in the sky, there remains the question as to whether the orientation was intentional or accidental. When a particular orientation is repeated at other monuments, as is the case with solstitial alignments, then the grounds for concluding its intentionality are increased.

Cairn G, Carrowkeel highlights the problems and contradictions of interpreting the veracity of a monument's orientation.[10] It is aligned roughly to the setting sun at the summer solstice, yet it is part of a group of monuments that are generally orientated to the north-west towards Cúil Irra and Knocknarea. It appears to have a roof-box type structure which admits the sun, but this type of construction is also found inside the chambers over recess entrances at other cairns in the complex, so it may equally just be a general construction technique (Fig. 4.1). From a technical point of view, Cairn G would not be considered sufficiently accurate to be a valid astronomical orientation, and yet the sun comes into the monument at sunset on the summer solstice, sometimes in a striking way. In recent years the sun's arrival in the chamber is awaited by groups that gather there every year on the evening of the summer solstice in the hope of witnessing the event; hence, though technically not a probable orientation, ritually it functions rather well. It is not inconceivable that the tradition of orientating monuments to the sun started in an unplanned way, perhaps at sites like Cairn G. Passage tomb builders may have been

*Figure 4.1. Beam of sunlight entering Cairn G, Carrowkeel
(photograph: author).*

more interested in approximate orientations than precise ones. It may also be that a greater interest in precision developed over time as more astronomically orientated monuments were constructed. Perhaps in the beginning, a particular part of the sun's journey or part of the sky was of importance from a mythic perspective, and the desire to orientate passage tombs more precisely was only a later refinement.

That astronomical orientations exist in the Irish passage tomb tradition seems indisputable. It is unnecessary to look to other regions for the inspiration to create astronomically aligned monuments. It seems the percentage of astronomically orientated passage tombs in Ireland is greater than that in other passage tomb regions. Indeed, other areas, such as Anglesey and the Orkney Islands, may have taken the tradition of astronomically orientating monuments from Ireland. The evidence suggests the investment of considerable energy and cumulative knowledge in this aspect of monument construction in Ireland.

One reason Newgrange is considered the astronomical monument *par excellence* is because its alignment occurs over a short period, only five or six days (although 5000 years ago the sun would have entered the chamber for one week on either side of the solstice). The length and narrowness of the passage demonstrate that great refinement had been achieved in this aspect of passage tomb construction. At other astronomically orientated passage tombs, alignment appears to be a more imprecise art, something that was perhaps worked at and gradually perfected. At Bryn Celli Ddu, a low ledge was found along one side of the passage interior in the course of excavation. This ledge has been re-interpreted as the base of a dry-stone wall used to narrow and hone the beam of sunlight entering the chamber.[11] One can only assume that an element of trial and error was present in the construction of monuments with astronomical features, and perhaps modifications of various kinds would, on occasion, have been necessary to achieve the desired end such as the closing stone across the passage entrance and roof-box as at Newgrange. At Maeshowe, the door-stone was 35 cm too short to fill the passage opening and therefore may have acted in a similar fashion to a roof-box.[12]

Notably, when the roof-box at Newgrange was uncovered, a quartz block was found wedged on one side of it (Fig. 4.2). A second quartz block appeared to have fallen from its original position in the roof-box into the passage. Unfortunately, both stones are now lost, but scratch marks on the floor of the roof-box indicated that they were repeatedly taken in and out. These stones or other contrivances may have allowed the keepers of the monument to exercise control over when the light entered the chamber; perhaps on all but a few chosen days, or to maintain complete darkness outside of those days. Features such as these may have compensated for less accurate arrangements or enhanced the drama of the event by limiting the days in which the sun would enter.

Figure 4.2. Roof-box at Newgrange (photograph: author).

The existence of a tradition of solar alignment of passage tombs begs other questions: when and why did this tradition start? What motivated Neolithic communities to chart the yearly journey of the sun? One factor may have been a fascination with the powers of growth and fertility (Chapter Three). Another factor may have been climatic changes that occurred in Ireland over the period when most passage tombs were constructed (Chapter Two). As noted previously, there is no evidence of astronomical orientation at Type 1 sites; it seems to be something that became important over time, perhaps in parallel with deterioration in the climate. Neolithic people may have been concerned with a perceived decline in the sun's light or power. Perhaps astronomically orientated chambers facilitated observation of the sun on its journey through the year, so that changes in the appearance of the light could be observed. Particular significance may have been placed on whether the sun appeared in the chamber on a seasonally important day, or to occasions when it failed to enter the chamber.

Meditation on light

It is difficult to appreciate just how influential the sun, moon and stars were for Neolithic communities. Part of the problem is our modern world separation from natural cycles. Since 2008, for the first time in human history a greater number of people live in urban than rural areas.[13] Fewer people work directly with nature to produce food. The question could be posed whether people living in our current technologically advanced and heavily electrified environment have the capacity to quantify the importance of the sky and seasons for people who lived in such radically different day-to-day settings? The turning seasons, weather, and seasonal cycles of growth and decay in the vegetative world would have influenced almost every aspect of the daily lives – and hence beliefs – of the communities that built Newgrange. Yet we rarely give significant weight to this in our analysis of astronomically orientated passage tombs. Most often it is suggested that astronomical orientations were used by elites to demonstrate and justify their authority. Astronomical alignments may also have served to place a monument in time, empowering it with special meanings on certain regular occasions, or helped to affirm its place at the centre of cosmic events.[14]

Typically, accounts of passage tomb orientations tend to focus on technicalities of the phenomena rather than trying to understand why people were aligning monuments towards the sun and what it meant to them. In particular, there has been an absence of a multi-sensory approach and qualitative aspect to the solar event. At Newgrange, it is clear that solar-orientated passage tombs may have been concerned with much more than a straightforward demonstration of engineering ability or astronomical expertise. On the contrary, these events may have been intended to be experienced in and for themselves. Anne Marie Moroney has highlighted other aspects of sun's light in her dedicated recording of sunlight in the chamber at Dowth South, over the period from November to February:

> The colour of the sun shining into this circular chamber and
> onto the stones is a bright beam at the beginning of this solar

pattern in winter. The light turns to a warm yellow and around the time of the solstice changes to a golden pink colour. As the days lengthen again the sun's rays are more honey-coloured and then become a bright, white light in February.[15]

The tone and character of the sun's light is constantly changing in the annual cycle; the color tones of high summer are not the same as those of autumn or mid-winter. The purpose of certain astronomically orientated monuments may have been the active ritual use of chambered cairns in terms of the direct observation of sunlight. Creating an alignment may not have been an end in itself. Instead, it may have been a means to witness and engage (or communicate) with a natural but mysterious phenomenon in a controlled ritual context. The construction of an astronomically aligned chambered cairn would have allowed this engagement to happen in a much more focused way than would have ordinarily been the case. Timothy Ingold has suggested that as a result of the Western world's fixation on the visual over the other senses, most of us have, "effectively lost touch with the experience of light".[16] How captivating it must have been for people at sites such as Newgrange to engage with and examine a small piece of the sun at close quarters on important days in the sun's cycle.

It is unlikely that prehistoric people viewed light as inanimate or a purely material phenomenon. Light moves and has warmth. The quality and tone of the light is constantly changing as the solstice event occurs. Furthermore, different atmospheric/weather conditions in any given year would have created dissimilar sunsets and sunrises. A heavy frost would create particular effects in the sky and result in colours in the chamber particular to those conditions. These differences may also have been keenly noted by the observers within the monuments. In this sense it may have been seen as a living entity with its own volition.

It may be that the observation of sunlight preceded an interest in calendrical time as a concern for passage tomb communities. This could provide an additional explanation for monuments with seemingly less than accurate alignments. Time keeping, and hence concomitantly precise alignments, were not the reason for their construction; rather the main concern was the observance of light.

Even today, for all our scientific knowledge, a mere representation of the sun can have a powerful affect. Olafur Eliasson's recreation of a sun in the Tate Modern in 2003–4 was very revealing in this regard.[17] Many visitors spontaneously lay down on the ground, basking in the glow of an entirely artificial solar orb (it did not give off any heat) (Plate 6). Another of his works, entitled *Your Sun Machine*, plays upon the movement of sunlight in a room.[18] The installation space was essentially empty, with a large hole in the roof. The piece invites viewers to contemplate the relationship between themselves, the sun, and the earth. Curator Susan May described the event as such:

> Each morning, sunlight streamed into the space through this aperture, creating an initially elliptical, then circular outline on the walls and floor of the space. As the day progressed, the beam of light shifted across the room, seemingly appointed as the object of the work.[19]

May notes that Eliasson has stated his work allows the viewer to have an experience of, "seeing yourself sensing". This sensing is bodily, and yet promotes thoughtfulness about the nature of perception. People are aware of the mechanisms involved, so it is clear to them that the changes in perception they experience come from within themselves. In this way perception itself becomes an object of consciousness. The call to reflect on the interaction of sunlight, space and the individual seems to be fundamental to Eliasson's installation, and to the experience at Newgrange. Light can only be seen in interaction with space; it is the resistance of space that makes it apparent. Without Newgrange, the sunlight in the Boyne valley would not have been narrowed to a beam that could be observed in darkness at such close quarters. The construction and design of the passage tomb allowed that particular type of engagement.

At astronomically orientated passage tombs such as Newgrange, created space and the phenomena they capture are as one – they come alive through dependence on one another. But it is the human body that witnesses this engagement, which makes observations, that interprets. Fundamentally, humans are designed for perception and reflection in a way that no other species is. We are of nature, but we are the instrument that allows nature to reflect upon itself. Time is an essential component of the phenomenon too. For the person located within a chamber, the astronomical effect may only happen at one time of the year (if a solstitial orientation). At a deeper level time can be seen as a component of space. It is space that provides the frame for the elaboration of time. Change happens in relation to the physical, the corporeal. One could say space and time come together in a harmonious way in a monument aligned with the sun.

A solar orientation can be a profound consideration; a phenomenon that is philosophical in and of itself. Appreciation of the winter solstice alignment at Newgrange deepens when one is aware of it as part of a tradition; a lengthy engagement with sun, and time-worn consideration of its role in human life. For Neolithic people this engagement may have raised many questions about their world and the role of the sun in their lives.

CHAPTER FIVE

Where the River Meets the Sea

They have returned! A large salmon is carried from the river, up-hill to the decorated entrance. Its belly opened, filled with eggs; round, red-orange, like small suns. The elders announce life has come back to the river. Surely the sun will soon be reborn.

Archaeology is the primary means of exploring the past, and it employs a battery of scientific and theoretical approaches in order to do so. The discipline is especially good at investigating certain aspects of the past, most notably the age and morphology of ancient structures, past human diet and pathologies and so on. But many aspects of past leave little trace, in particular myths and beliefs and some ritual practices.[1] As our version/s of the past are largely determined by the scientific and interpretative techniques available, we can end-up with somewhat selectively framed histories. This chapter attempts to expand the narrative at Newgrange through investigating aspects of the lives of communities in the Boyne Valley for which there is only minimal archaeological data. Specifically, it explores the relationship between the Brú na Bóinne complex, the Boyne River and the sea; the appearance and disappearance of migratory creatures, especially the salmon; and how the rhythms of nature may have influenced ceremony and ritual at Newgrange.

Salmon and ceremony

Though somewhat under-theorised, the Boyne and the monuments held within its most famous bend are intimately related. As noted previously, Brú na Bóinne is in an island-like landscape setting, with the river and its tributaries creating an autonomous unit of land; effectively, Newgrange cannot be approached without crossing water. Of the three largest sites in the Bend of the Boyne, it is Newgrange that is most closely associated with the river (Plate 1). The Boyne can be seen from the entrance of Newgrange, but not from the entrances of nearby Knowth or Dowth. Newgrange is also the most visible and arguably the most dramatically situated of the three monuments as one travels upstream by boat.[2]

The Boyne together with its tributaries comprise nearly 600 km of river channel. The river may have been tidal up to the Bend of the Boyne during the Neolithic. Mitchell discovered blue-grey estuarine clay three metres deep near Glenmore House, about one kilometre upstream from Dowth (close to the most easterly point of the Bend of the Boyne before it continues its journey from Brú na Bóinne to the sea). Knowing that sea levels were four metres higher when the Boyne passage tombs were built, he realised that the tide (and hence estuarine matter) once progressed further west along the river than is the case today, potentially as far as Newgrange itself.[3]

This meeting place of sea and river would have been a hive of seasonal activity in the Neolithic, as it still is today. Cormorants, herons and kingfishers can be found along the river banks. In the winter months, flocks of whooper swans migrating from Iceland make their home in the fields adjacent to the Boyne overlooked by Newgrange.[4] Perhaps the most significant visitor however is the Atlantic salmon.

Much debate has taken place in recent years regarding changes in diet at the onset of the Neolithic. A considerable body of evidence now exists which demonstrates that marine resources were not significant in the diet of agricultural communities in Neolithic Ireland and Britain, including recent analysis at Knowth.[5] Salmon bones were not recovered during O'Kelly's excavation, but wet sieving was not a feature of excavation techniques at that time.[6] However, in subsequent excavations at the rear of Newgrange in the 1980s, the excavation director observed that, "Tiny fragments of fish bones were recorded amongst the plant macro remains suggesting exploitation of the plentiful fish supplies in the nearby river Boyne".[7] Both contexts where bones (species unidentified) were found are likely to be Neolithic in date. Indeed, one of the contexts was under the turf mound which lies within Newgrange's cairn. A radiocarbon date on other organic material from the same location suggests material from there is contemporary with the construction of Newgrange.[8]

Yet even if not a primary food source, it is unlikely that people in this area would have ignored the great migration of salmon up the Boyne River. The salmon runs on the Boyne would have represented a significant seasonal marker in the lives of these communities. Atlantic salmon (*Salmo salar*) can be found in the River Boyne at various times of the year. A spring run in March/April (primarily fish which have spent two winters at sea), a grilse run (one-sea-winter salmon) beginning in July, but also a spawning run in the late autumn/winter period. Today, the period after mid-November is particularly important as it is then salmon begin to run up the Boyne en route to spawning grounds in the river's many tributaries.[9] Salmon swim forward and back with the tides to the point where salt water meets fresh water waiting for the right time to enter the river on its spawning run.

The prime salmon fishing stretch of the river now (and probably in the past) was the stretch between the towns of Navan and Drogheda, in the middle of which lies the Bend of the Boyne. Visitors at the Brú na Bóinne Visitor Centre will sometimes see seals coming up the river from the sea in pursuit of salmon.[10] It is only around 19 km from Newgrange to the sea (not as the crow flies but as the river flows); salmon could have travelled that distance in a short time. Local knowledge suggests that if a salmon is seen 'showing' or 'pitching' in Navan, about 15 km upstream from Newgrange, then within three days salmon will be in their spawning streams (which can be up to 80 km from the coast). Typically, the salmon will run after a flood, a day or two after the soil and other debris of the flood wash has settled. Other factors influencing the salmon's run include water temperature, the length of the day and, interestingly, the angle of the sun.[11] Just as the renewal of the sun was vital to the community that built Newgrange, so too, it was vital to the salmon's successful return to the river where it was first spawned.

Through autumn, great quantities of fish gathered at the mouth of the river, east of Drogheda, waiting for the right conditions to begin their journey upstream for spawning. Female salmon already have eggs inside them as they begin this journey. Salmon would have moved with the tides, perhaps up to the Bend of the Boyne, until the necessary physiological changes had taken place in their bodies and the outer conditions were optimum for entering the fresh water. Today, the minimum number of spawning salmon required to maintain the population in the Boyne is 10,000.[12] Given the decline in fish populations in Britain and Ireland, however, beginning with the introduction of weirs, and then exacerbated by the rise in river pollution and intensive fishing of sea stocks, these population figures are only a fraction of what they once would have been.[13] We must imagine that the Boyne was thick with salmon. Currently, this spawning run takes place anywhere from mid-November to late January; it is, and would always have been, a winter affair. Significantly, the winter solstice falls almost precisely in the middle of this twelve-week period.

Salmon returning from the sea would have been more sought after than fish which had been in the river for longer periods. If returning salmon were fished, it was most likely at dusk or dawn: salmon move at night and hence so do salmon anglers. Salmon tend to rest in pools which would have been the best fishing locations, probably well-known to fishermen in the past. The ancient river channel would likely have had a few sudden drops where fish would accumulate. There is some evidence that in smaller river systems large salmon will choose the first suitable spawning habitat above the tidal limit.[14]

For many peoples around the world, the turning of the sun is considered the beginning of the New Year. This seasonal festival is usually perceived to be the primary reason for creating the winter solstice alignment at Newgrange. That may be only part of the story, however. Beyond a radical alteration in salmon migration patterns, we can assume that many salmon would have been moving up the

Boyne River before December 21. The salmon's life cycle mirrors the apparent death and rebirth of the sun; after spawning the vast majority of salmon die, but only after depositing the eggs that ensure the birth of the river's new salmon population.

The location of Newgrange implies that salmon runs would have been visible seasonal markers in the lives of Neolithic people. From the point of view of the Boyne Valley inhabitants – *before the sun returned, the salmon returned*. It is possible that the salmon were seen as heralds of the new year, returning with promises of abundance for the seasons to follow, just as was hoped for the sun. As everything was dying in the middle of winter, as the sun was coming to a standstill, the salmon were returning out of darkness, bearing promises of fecundity. Salmon usually pass waterfalls and other obstacles in daylight hours. This life-and-death struggle may have been seen as a visible emblem of strength or bravery, or as a sign of the irrepressible regenerative power of nature.

For the communities associated with Newgrange, the souls of the dead could have been imagined to make a similar journey to that of the salmon, departing or returning at the time of the winter solstice. The salmon's return may have been equated with the return of departed members of the human community and the appearance of the gods or mythical ancestors in the winter solstice ceremonies. One wonders was the journey of the salmon likened to the transformation of people who sat within the darkened passage tomb chambers. Or perhaps tribal elders or ritual specialists equated themselves with the salmonoid ancestors, perceiving their role, like the salmon's, to be heralds and mediators of this great cosmological event.

The timing of the salmon's spawning run could have been ideologically significant, perhaps connected with the solar rituals that took place over the winter solstice period at Newgrange. One wonders whether ceremonies were held to safeguard the return of the salmon as was the case for many of the peoples of the Northern Pacific Rim.[15] Communities in the Boyne Valley may have anticipated the re-entering of the salmon into the river, as a signal for the beginning of winter ceremonies. Though the winter solstice event tends to be seen as primarily or exclusively about the sun, it is not inconceivable that the salmon and the river in which they spawned were an equally integral part of the solstice celebrations.

Coastal journeys

As noted in Chapter One, most Type 1 Irish passage tombs occur in coastal locations. Many other passage tombs while not coastal appear to be intentionally sited close to rivers, perhaps as a way of maintaining a connection to the coast. Even without this information it would be possible to infer a strong connection between Newgrange and the sea (Fig. 5.1). For instance, the Newry granodiorite and Mourne granite cobbles used to decorate the entrance at Newgrange are likely to have been collected from beaches on the north shore of Dundalk Bay, some 40 km north-east. Equally striking is that the white vein quartz used in the façade is thought to have been gathered from the Wicklow Mountains, 70 km to the south-east (though recent work by George Sevastopulo indicates that the nearer site of Rockabill Island may have been another source).[16] If Wicklow quartz were brought by boat, it would have required Neolithic people to sail down the Boyne River, out into the Boyne Estuary at Drogheda, southwards down the Irish coast to Wicklow, and land somewhere that would have allowed the collection of quartz. Then they would have had to return along the same route with a significantly heavier boat. If Rockabill Island is proven as a source, it provides undeniable proof that the Boyne Valley communities undertook sea journeys.

The movement of quartz, granites and granodiorite no doubt represents a considerable feat. Yet it seems more feasible than the mammoth task of transporting the monument's primary construction stones. If the two to five tonne greywacke kerbstones and multiple additional construction stones of similar weight were brought from Clogher Head by boat, as has been suggested, it implies that the builders of Newgrange were not only capable of boat travel, but were experts on the water, skilled enough to take on treacherous journeys by sea.

To put this in context, the total weight of the ninety seven stones

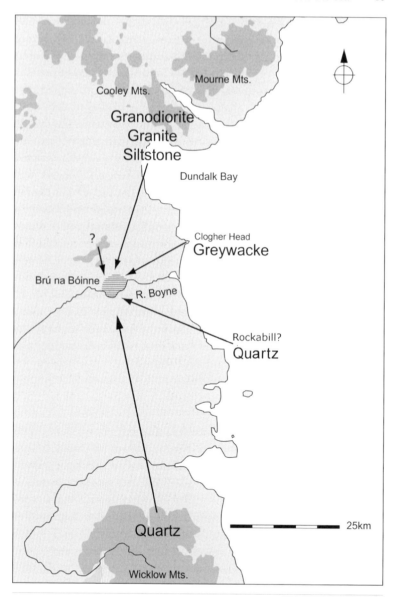

Figure 5.1. Materials transported to Newgrange (after Cooney 2000, fig. 5.2).

used in the Newgrange kerb is estimated to be three hundred tonnes.[17] The coastal Clogher Head and Little Harbour Lower Palaeozoic foundations from which Adrian Phillips and Mary Corcoran deduced these greywacke stones were quarried is approximately 16 km north-east of Newgrange as the crow flies.[18] Sevastopulo, who has made the most recent evaluation, is of the opinion that transportation by boat was the method used to retrieve those stones. He has also discovered that some of the geologically less typical construction stones used at Newgrange were sourced near Slane, Co. Meath.[19] Water transport from Clogher Head would have involved a seven kilometre trip southwards from the coastal quarry site to the mouth of the Boyne, followed by a further 20 km of river travel. Geraldine and Matthew Stout have proposed that these huge stones were strapped under boats at the low tide and the subsequent rising tide used to lift the whole, an enormous and technically complex task.[20] Further research is required along the coast or in the river channel to see if evidence of failed journeys such as dropped stones can be identified. However, a dropped stone was tentatively identified by Adrian Phillips using geophysical techniques, and greywacke slabs have been seen on the floor of the river bed and at one of the fish weirs by local builder and researcher of ancient boats Claidhbh Ó Gibne.[21]

Cockles and mussels

The evidence seems to indicate that Boyne Valley communities were journeying to the coast to retrieve large construction stones. Conor Brady's lithic distributions and raw material acquisition survey suggests people also travelled to the coast for smaller materials, especially sought after pebble flint, which came from shingle beaches in Counties Louth, Meath or Dublin.[22] A fresh crop of stone would have appeared on these beaches following each storm event. Additionally, tentative artefactual evidence from inside the monuments further suggests the sea as something present in the lives and worldview of passage tomb communities, in particular the marine shells recorded in all four major passage tomb complexes.

At Newgrange, nine fragments of seashell were found, representing five different species.[23] Some of these shells may have entered the site with sand from the coast used as stone packing material, as O'Kelly surmised. Additionally, a number of oyster and scallop shells were found at Fourknocks, Co. Meath, 15 km south-east of Newgrange, including a perforated shell that was probably part of a personal ornament.[24] A considerable heap of shells was found under the cairn of the passage tomb at Knocklea in Rush, Co. Dublin. A layer of periwinkle shells around 20 cm thick, interspersed with limpet and mussel shells was discovered the mound surrounding the chamber.[25] Though Michael Herity interpreted these shells as forming part of the construction, Finbar McCormick has suggested that it is more likely that the megalith was built over a pre-existing shell midden.[26] Either way, the builders would have been aware of them.

At Loughcrew, two hundred and sixty five cockle, periwinkle, pecten, limpet and mussel shells and one hundred white sea-pebbles were discovered in Cairn H in the late nineteenth century.[27] The location is significant as Loughcrew is over 60 km inland. The evidence is complicated by Iron Age use of the site, however, in particular the occurrence of numerous bone flakes with Iron Age La Tène style decoration.[28] Marine shells have been found at many of Carrowmore passage tombs, including mussels, oysters, pecten, and cardium. A large pit full of shells was found at Carrowmore 7. This find is of particular interest because the shells – mussels and oysters – were mostly unopened, suggesting to the excavation director that this deposition was a religious offering.[29] Only a single marine shell was recorded in 1911 at Carrowkeel, in Cairn H, but the excavations were rushed and much evidence may have been missed or discarded.[30]

Shells have regularly been found in chambered tombs in Britain, especially on the eastern side of the Irish Sea.[31] Shells have also been noted from at least two of the Welsh passage tombs, Bryn Celli Ddu and Bryn Yr Hen Bobl.[32] The shells found at Barclodiad y Gawres in Wales were in a particularly interesting context, covering the remains of a concoction involving amphibian, fish, snake, and eel bones.[33]

If passage tomb communities perceived passage tombs as otherworld places, how would this sense of the monuments have been expressed; how would such expression show up in the archaeological record? One way would be to demonstrate that the monuments were places where conventional rules no longer applied, or where conventional reality was somehow reversed. Introducing objects from the sea into the monuments may have demonstrated that these were places where conventional reality was upended or reversed; where this-world rules no longer applied. Another method of achieving this would be to use parts of sea creatures to create ritual equipment, or even perhaps to depict them.

Creatures of the deep

The many whalebone finds from Carrowmore provide yet another link to the sea. These objects include long pins fashioned from whale bone (species unidentified) found at Carrowmore. One example from Carrowmore 15 was 50 cm long.[34] Of further interest are unusual circular objects made from sperm whale teeth from several of the Carrowmore tombs (Fig. 5.2).[35]

Still today, regular whale sightings take place off the Sligo coast near Carrowmore, and whales occasionally become stranded in the area. One wonders what the Neolithic communities thought of these monsters of the sea; did they feature in their stories and myths? However they were understood, it is probable that beached animals would have garnered considerable attention; and considerable excitement could have been generated as valuable parts of the animal claimed or portioned out.

Whalebone has also been recorded in association with chambered cairns in the Orkney Islands.[36] At Ibister and Point of Cott, whale parts were used to make necklaces. The whales teeth used at Point of Cott indicate three different species of whale (sperm whale, killer whale and pilot whale). Serge Cassen and others have proposed that certain pieces of art on menhirs in Brittany (known as *hache-charrue*) which in the past were construed as axes may be representations of sperm whales.[37] Though not considered as such previously, a seldom

Figure 5.2. Whalebone objects from Carrowmore (photograph © National Museum of Ireland. Photographer Bryan Routledge).

photographed piece of art from the inaccessible western passage tomb nearby at Knowth might similarly have represented a cetaceous creature (Plate 7 and Fig 5.3). The piece, which is fashioned in relief, is atypical of passage tomb art which is more usually focused around a relatively defined set of geometric motifs.

The design in question occupies an important place in the Knowth construction, being located at the end of the undifferentiated western tomb. It could be considered the 'showpiece' of the chamber area. The outer layer of the stone has been assiduously picked away to leave the design in relief. Remnants of an earlier carving has been incorporated into the right-hand extremity of the depiction, making it possible the relief carving was executed in a phase of re-modification. These earlier carvings include a series of lozenges on the tail-like projection to the right and some angular lines in the central part of the image. A long triangular shape that projects down from the image and points towards a prominent hollow/solution hole in the stone, could resemble a large pectoral fin.

If this artwork were intended to be a representation of a whale

Figure 5.3. Close-up of art from the chamber of the western tomb at Knowth with outline of possible humpback whale carving (photograph after Ken Williams).

or dolphin, can it be identified as a particular species? The absence of a dorsal fin would seem to preclude dolphin as a possibility. The upper line above the main figure may depict the spray of water and mist emitted by whales. It may be significant that of seventeen species of whale recorded from Irish waters, only three – the minke whale, northern bottlenose whale and humpback whale – have been confirmed along the east coast in the modern era. Humpback whales (*Megaptera novaeangliae*) are migratory, appearing in Irish waters in late summer, autumn and winter (especially off the south-west coast). We do not know much of the Neolithic distribution of whale species but we can say with some degree of certainty that humpback whales occurred in the Irish Sea at that time, as they do today, but most likely in greater numbers.[38]

The humpback whale is enormous (up to 40 tonnes). The largest can measure five metres in diameter. Besides its size it has additional features which are helpful in distinguishing it from other whale species. These features could be central to identifying the potential cretaceous species represented in the Knowth art. Firstly, and perhaps crucially, the humpback has a uniquely long white pectoral fin. Their pectoral fin is proportionally larger than any other cetacean and thus is referred to as the 'winged' whale. This is reflected in its Latin name *Megaptera* (*Mega*: big, *ptera*: wing). Secondly, it has a small rather indistinct dorsal fin, set two-thirds of the way along its back. Thirdly, it has defined tail flukes with pointed ends (unlike several other whale species). Of the large whales frequently recorded in Irish waters, they are the only species to commonly raise their tail in the air before deep diving, which proves a particularly useful identifier. Finally, humpbacks are noticeable for creating significant upward projections of spray as they propel air through their blowholes. These fountains can reach a height of about three metres. The spray can be a defining feature as well: humpback spray is vertical, unlike some other whale species (*e.g.*, sperm whale, which blows its spray forward and to the left).[39]

If each of these characteristics of the humpback whale is compared with the Knowth carving, some significant points of correspondence

Figure 5.4. (Left) Humpback whale. Note the long downward-pointing pectoral fin and the defined tail flukes (iStock.com/freestylephoto).

can be observed (Fig. 5.4). The potential whale depicted in the Knowth art is noticeable for the long triangular downward pointing relief section, which might be interpreted as a depiction of a long pectoral fin.[40] Of all cetaceans the scale of this 'fin' could only be compared with the uniquely long pectoral fin of the humpback whale. The species is noted for its acrobatics, which include pectoral fin slapping.

No dorsal fin is depicted, which would be appropriate as this is such an indistinct feature of the Humpback, as opposed to other whale species. As to the tail area, quite defined flukes have been created by the carver. The material around the points of the tail has been delicately removed to leave two slender extremities. Again, the shape created by the carver would appear to suggest that a humpback-type tail was the artist's target. If the image in question is of a whale, then the tail in this instance is depicted in a downward thrashing motion. This, again, is a feature of humpback acrobatic displays (known as 'lobtailing'), when whales repeatedly slap their tails down on the water surface.

Lastly, in the Knowth image an upward line, or rather a strip of uncarved stone, appears approximately above where a whale blowhole would be. This ribbon of stone must have been significant to the carver as he/she went to great lengths to remove the material on either side to allow this feature to be present. It seems to depict the ejection of spray that these creatures are known for. In terms of the four primary identifying features of the humpback whale outlined here (long pectoral fin, indistinct dorsal, pointed tail extremities, and spray), it would appear that all four resonate with the Knowth West chamber carving.

A special attribute of humpback whales, perhaps the one for which they are most famed, is their complex 'songs'. Though the songs are best heard underwater, it is possible that Neolithic communities who travelled along the east coast of Ireland may have heard these songs (they are sometimes heard today through the hulls of boats). Given the dramatic jets of spray they produce, and their sheer size, it can be assumed that these creatures would have been one of the most noticed, and presumably marvelled at, creatures in prehistory. They would have been the largest creature in the world of the people who built Newgrange.

Would they have been seen at close proximity as the monument builders travelled up or down the east coast sourcing materials for the construction of Newgrange? It may be significant that the headland at Clogher Head, where the Newgrange construction stones came from, is today one of the primary whale sighting points along the east coast. Reported sightings of cetaceans in Irish waters have increased dramatically in the last few years as the population recovers, including confirmed sightings of humpback whales in the Irish Sea from the coast of counties Down, Louth and Dublin. Significantly, one of the rare east coast sightings includes a recent confirmed report of a humpback north-east of Rockabill Island; *i.e.*, the same location where some of the Newgrange quartz is believed to have been retrieved. The whale was sighted around 10 km from the mouth of the Boyne River.[41]

That the Knowth relief carving may be a depiction of a whale is an intriguing possibility and, if true, would certainly alter our perception of the communities who constructed Newgrange and Knowth and their relationship with the sea. It would also mean a radical change in our understanding of passage tomb art as something with potential for greater amounts of representative elements than previously considered (and thus more in line with megalithic art on the Continent). Though

Irish passage tomb art is usually considered non-representative, there is nothing definitive that says it was necessarily considered that way in the Neolithic.[42] A thoroughgoing comparative examination by Robin has identified real world items that seem to have been depicted by Neolithic carvers including snakes, trees and symbolic representations of tomb architectural features.[43]

Yet we must remain cautious. The propensity of the mind to seek the familiar in the unfamiliar and representation in abstraction is well known. Renowned scholar of ancient Irish art Peter Harbison once noted that he fondly imagined the same piece of art at Knowth as a bear with a running nose![44] Moreover, in Brittany, where art depicting whales has been postulated, many examples can be compared, and evidence of a tradition around that specific design is apparent. Nevertheless, if the Knowth art is a depiction of a whale, the artistic form is of a much less abstracted variety than the possible examples in Brittany. Indeed, it would appear that in this case abstract geometric art has been removed or obliterated to allow a relatively realistic depiction to be completed.

At Brú na Bóinne many things came together: a sacred island separated from the world by rivers, a necessary crossing over water, and powerful seasonal events: the return of salmon and the rebirth of the sun. Surely this place apart would have had meanings and associations different from those of the surrounding landscape. It is hard to conceive that the area was not considered a focal point of religious activity and supernatural belief. The winter solstice story at Newgrange is one of rebirth and return, but perhaps not just of the sun as it is normally characterised, but of the River Boyne and of the fish population within it; of winter birds from unknown lands, of seeds stirring under the ground as ceremonies took place, and of the return of ancestors and departed souls to bolster and increase in the human population for the coming year. By considering these elements together we can perhaps extend our typical archaeological narratives and imagine that for Neolithic people, Newgrange, and perhaps the whole island landscape on which the Brú na Bóinne monuments sit, was a hugely evocative religious centre, a place of powerful multivalent seasonal symbolism and associations.

CHAPTER SIX

Going Public

Walking the road of the gods, towards the Brú, shining. The anointed one holds aloft a staff, surmounted by a magnificent stone macehead. Great crowds look on in awe.

When Irish passage tombs are examined at an island-wide level, it becomes clear that Newgrange was founded upon a series of progressive developments which occurred over quite a long-lived period. The new dates from Carrowmore imply that those developments began over four or five hundred years before sunlight poured into Newgrange's cold chamber that first winter solstice morning. This gradual evolution is evident not only in the increasing size of the monuments, but in new design features, in styles of passage tomb art, in the greater precision achieved in astronomical orientation, and in the more accomplished craftsmanship found in the artefacts and furnishings from passage tomb chambers. A major change with respect to the role of the monuments can be discerned around the middle of the fourth millennium BC: it appears that ancestral burial rites in early Type 1 passage tombs give way to internal ritual in larger Type 2 passage tombs, sites suitable for human entry. In this chapter, another major transformation in the construction and role of these monuments is introduced. Passage tombs begin to incorporate design features intended for public consumption. Display seems to become tremendously important: platforms around the cairn exterior, large external art, exotic and elaborate ritual equipment, and a probable elite are all features of this late and spectacular outgrowth of the passage tomb tradition. Newgrange is representative of this change, as are Knowth and Dowth and a limited number of passage tombs elsewhere in Ireland. These, Type 3, passage tombs are constructed towards the end of the passage tomb tradition, from approximately 3200 to 3000 BC.

Resplendent rites

In terms of the scale and sophistication of design, the last quarter of the fourth millennium BC was a high-point of passage tomb construction. Invariably these passage tombs are exceptionally large, some with diameters over 50 m. They also tend to provide evidence of ritual paraphernalia not found at other passage tombs. As well as the increasing diameter of the monuments and volume of the cairn, other architectural features increase in scale, too. Larger stones are used in the chamber construction, longer kerbstones are sourced, passages reach greater lengths and corbelled roofs are considerably higher. Nevertheless, some passage tombs though not of great size, may have many of the features associated with this stage of passage tomb construction; for instance, sites such as Knockroe and Baltinglass (see below).

Unsurprisingly, this late flourish in the passage tomb tradition also produces the most architecturally complex monuments; a host of additional design features and modifications are present. It appears these changes were conceived with public ceremony in mind. Features that were once only associated with internal ritual are now found outside, employed in external ritual and ceremony. It is almost as if the monuments had been turned inside-out. The exterior of the sites take on particular importance, including procession around the cairn and possible routeways to the monument. External design changes include:

- Straightened façade
- Platform (extending from the cairn)
- Quartz (as part of external construction)
- Stone settings
- Flat-topped cairn
- Kerbstone art
- Linear monuments (leading to the monument)

Straightened façade: This is one of most recognisable public-oriented design modifications. Where once a monument's façade was curved, it now appears straightened, particularly around the entrance area. At Newgrange, the straightened façade may have been designed to highlight rituals conducted in front of the monument.[1] It may also have better facilitated the construction of walls or other revetted elements above the kerb-line.[2] An interesting feature of Newgrange is the open area between the passage entrance and the kerb, behind K1, the profusely decorated entrance stone. The modern reconstruction emphasises this area, but even in the monument's original state people could have gathered there. It may have been intended that a person or persons would be seen in that potent location by groups assembled in front of the monument, perhaps for a final ritual previous to entering the passage.

Platform: These low circular features extend outwards from the cairn perimeter. Significant platforms are found at Knowth, Knockroe, and Carns Hill West and Listoghil. Platforms are another way of emphasising the external part of the monument. These features may have been used as stages for ceremony or performances, providing an architectural distinction between the performers and onlookers. At Newgrange, some of the white quartz discovered around the cairn during excavations could have formed a platform or, more likely on recent evidence, at some point in the monument's history have been taken from the cairn to create a platform, but the interpretation of that evidence is much debated.[3]

Quartz: It seems quartz was very significant to people over the whole period of passage tomb construction. The earliest passage tombs have quartz associated with them, usually found inside their chambers.[4] However, the use of quartz seems to have become more important over time, particularly so on the outside of developed passage tombs. Large quantities of quartz were recorded not only at Newgrange, but also at Knowth, Cairn T Loughcrew, Baltinglass Hill and Knockroe. The quartz façade around the entrance to Newgrange is not only striking when witnessed from within the monument, but when seen from outside, especially around mid-winter when struck by beams of morning sunlight. Interestingly, the quartz at Newgrange was not found around the whole monument but only half way around, either side of the entrance. The intention was not simply to decorate the monument, but that it would have a dramatic effect on a viewing public.

Stone Settings: These circular or semi-circular features, usually found on either side of the entrance, were another way of enhancing the visual impact and prestige of a passage tomb. At Newgrange, a large stone setting (4×3.4 m) was uncovered to the east of the passage entrance. This contained approximately six hundred water-rolled quartz pebbles, one hundred granite boulders and more than six hundred fragments of quarried angular quartz. The eastern and western tombs at Knowth had a combined total of thirteen stone settings placed outside the passage entrances. Though unexcavated, stone settings are also apparent at Queen Maeve's tomb and at Loughcrew, Cairn T.[5]

Flat-topped cairn: The flat-topped cairn design is another of the more notable features at Newgrange and later passage tombs. This design is found at Queen Maeve's tomb, Carns Hill West, as well as at Knowth, Dowth and Newgrange. The flat area on top of Newgrange is 32 m in diameter. This design would have facilitated gatherings on the top of the monuments in a way that dome-shaped cairns or cairns with angular apexes could not. This design modification may have developed as a response to the large gatherings below, perhaps permitting important figures or speakers to be seen or heard by crowds from a distance.

Kerbstone art: An important defining feature of this stage of passage tomb construction is that the monuments became the foci of rituals and ceremonies engaged in or viewed by the public. One indicator of this change is the occurrence of kerbstone art. It is notable that the art found on the kerbstones is often larger and more complex than the carvings inside the monuments. For example, the triple spiral inside Newgrange is barely one third the size of the similar example on the entrance stone outside the passage.[6] At Knowth the motifs on the kerbstones are exceptionally large, as is the scalariform motif on the kerb at Heapstown Cairn. This suggests kerbstone art may have been intended to be viewed by observers from a distance.

As art appears externally at these sites, a number of archaeologists have proposed that it may point to public procession around the monuments.[7] At Knowth, the size and quantity of the art on the kerbstones might indicate procession and movement around the stones were an element in the rituals performed there. George Eogan has suggested that:

> One might visualise a morning ceremony on the east side, and an evening ceremony on the west side. Such rites could have been the occasion of a pan-passage-tomb festival involving people from far and wide ... Part of the event may have involved an enactment of ritual outside the tomb, for instance a procession around the mound, taking advantage of the decoration on the kerbstones.[8]

No art has been found on the stones of the boulder circles at Carrowmore. Only one decorated kerb is recorded at the Carrowkeel complex, and three from the Loughcrew complex.[9] It is telling that eighteen of the nineteen monuments with kerbstone art are in Leinster in the east and thirteen of those are in the Brú na Bóinne complex. A great many kerbstones are decorated at the main sites at Knowth and Newgrange. Art is found on the visible faces of forty kerbstones at Newgrange alone, as well as on kerbstones at Sites K and L adjacent to Newgrange.

Linear monuments and procession: The ceremonies which took place at Newgrange and elsewhere at Brú na Bóinne may not only have incorporated enhanced external features and movement around the monuments, but public processions through the landscape too. Unexcavated linear cursus-like sites sometimes occur near passage tomb complexes, for instance, at Loughcrew.[10] These linear monuments have traditionally been seen as Late Neolithic in date. They are quite variable in form, however, and may be equally variable in date. For this reason, it should not be automatically assumed that they were in use at the same time as passage tombs. Even so, some examples could be materialisations of earlier processional ways (for instance, timber-lined avenues). It may be significant though that the cursus-like monument at Newgrange is roughly on the same alignment as the main mound.[11] Equally, the cursus monument at Tara (known as the Banqueting Hall) is aligned directly on the Mound of the Hostages. Hence, in these two instances at least, cursus-like monuments may be aligned in relation with the passage tomb, if in different ways. The construction of the 65 m long-barrow at Ballinacrad (Site G) to the south south-west of Dowth is another example of a connection between a linear earthwork and a passage tomb.[12] Additionally, four cursus monuments in south Leinster, at least two of which (Keadeen and Knockeiran/Rathnabo, Co. Wicklow) are directly associated with stone cairns, both possible passage tombs.[13]

Processional routeways underscore a desire to influence the way that groups move through the landscape. They create drama by controlling how and when groups see a monument. It seems that initial invisibility of the cairn, followed by their dramatic appearance, was one aim of this intricate landscape choreography. This dramatic intent in a landscape context is in keeping with what seems to be one of the overall design objectives in this phase of passage tomb construction: the visual impact of the monument. Everything was about display, from the shock factor as the monument appears in one's visual range for the first time, the awe engendered by its scale, the striking colour contrasts created through the selective use of materials, and not least the evocative and mysterious art decorating its exterior.

Prestige artefacts

The external aspects of the monument tell us a lot about the changes in passage tomb ritual, especially with regard to the desire to engage with larger groups. The objects found inside the monuments can also

*Figure 6.1. Stone balls of varying scales from Loughcrew. Display case,
National Museum of Ireland (photograph: author).*

contribute to understanding changes in ritual focus. A defined set of artefacts occur in Irish passage tombs, usually found in association with cremated or unburnt human bone. These include pendants and beads, bone or antler pins, balls of stone and baked clay, sherds of pottery referred to as 'Carrowkeel ware' and quartz.

Notably, passage tomb finds appear to increase in the size and craftsmanship over time, mirroring the evolution in sophistication of monuments. At Carrowmore and Carrowkeel, stone balls typically measure around one centimetre in diameter, whereas as at the Loughcrew and Brú na Bóinne complexes, larger examples and/or examples made from exotic materials occur. Two particularly fine examples from Loughcrew are displayed in the National Museum of Ireland (Fig. 6.1). The largest, from Cairn F, is almost eight centimetres in diameter and made from ironstone; the other, found in Cairn L, is approximately seven centimetres and fashioned from grey marble. Both were highly polished and show no sign of wear.[14] At Newgrange it is possible that the more spectacular finds were removed by antiquarians and other early visitors. Fortunately, two unusual serpentine balls remained to be discovered during O'Kelly excavations. This striking green stone is rare in Ireland, though native sources were available.

Unusual 'prestige' objects are also associated with this third phase of passage tomb construction. Some of these artefacts may not have been connected with the cremation pyre or funerary ritual, but instead reflect wider, non-burial, ceremony. Examples include atypical finds such as the sandstone 'phallus' found in a stone setting at Newgrange, and the baetyls and maceheads found at Knowth. The finely worked macehead from the eastern chamber displayed no evidence of burning and, significantly, was placed by itself in the chamber, and not mixed with human remains (Fig. 6.2). The object appears to have been deliberately sealed by a deposit of loose shale.[15] Objects such as this may have had an active role in religious events, in this case perhaps surmounting a staff, or associated with a person or ceremonial role of some significance. Ceremonies which took place at Type 3 passage tombs may have been given additional splendour through the employment of this unique and exotic ritual equipment. Presumably there were people who used this equipment, a sacerdotal group of some description. We can only imagine what other ritual equipment once existed; for instance, special items of clothing.

Foremost among the items of specialised ritual equipment are the stone 'basins' which occur in some Irish passage tombs. Several of the finely wrought basin stones could also be considered exotic or prestigious, especially if the stone came from a distant location. Notably, the upper basin from the right recess at Newgrange is composed of granite from the Mourne Mountains 40–50 km to the north. In a recent analysis, a total of twenty-five stones from sixteen monuments were adjudged to be basin stones.[16] Only four sites – Newgrange, Knowth, Slieve Gullion and Loughcrew Cairn L – have more than one basin present. Twenty of the twenty-five stone basins

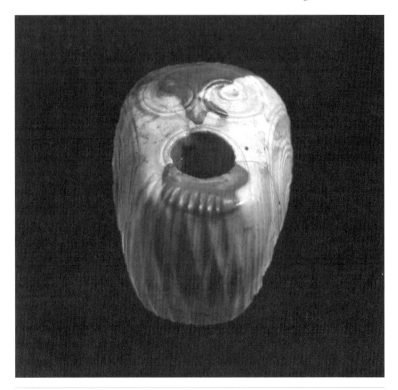

Figure 6.2. Ovoid macehead, Knowth East (photograph: Ken Williams).

are in Loughcrew and the Brú na Bóinne complexes. Significantly, none are known from the Carrowmore or Carrowkeel complexes or in any other passage tomb in the west of Ireland; yet another indication that the western complexes did not see the late developments which occurred elsewhere. They appear to be particularly associated with passage tombs in the eastern part of the island – a feature of the late flourishing of design and innovation which occurred towards the end of the passage tomb tradition.

Of the two basins in the eastern recess at Newgrange, the upper granite example is particularly finely finished (Fig. 6.3). It has two

Figure 6.3. Basin stones from the east recess at Newgrange (photograph: Ken Williams).

distinctive circular depressions on the upper part of the inner surface. Given the size of these Brú na Bóinne examples they are better ascribed to the architecture of the site than as artefacts; in several instances their bulk precludes mobility. Though damaged in the past, the carved example from Knowth East is one of the most stunning items from the Irish Neolithic. It is notable that it was so large that it may have had to be put in position and the recess built around it.[17] As Sheridan has noted, these basins are not just well made versions of the more usual basin stones; they fall into an entirely different class.[18]

Though some basins required considerable work to shape, the final product would not have been visible to most people. They may be another indicator that the religious role of Type 3 passage tombs had changed. At sites where basins fill the recesses Type 2 passage tomb ritual, as described in previous chapters, could no longer have occurred. That role may have already been adequately served by Type 2 passage tombs surrounding the focal sites in the wider complex, however. We know that modest passage tombs were still erected after the construction of the main mound at Knowth and Newgrange, so clearly the smaller less sophisticated sites could fulfil a function not served by their larger neighbours.

Changes in the design and scale of passage tombs, together with the more accomplished artefacts within their chambers, are indicators of a second fault-line within the passage tomb tradition. Secretive rituals at isolated locations have given way to ceremonies concerned with public display and religious spectacle.

Other Newgranges?

Newgrange is an exceptional site. Bar its sister sites in the Boyne Valley, Knowth and Dowth, there are no passage tombs in Ireland with which it can be compared in terms of scale. Yet it also represents a stage of passage tomb construction, and several other sites also have some similar features. In total there are ten passage tombs with cairns with diameters above 50 m, many of which may be Type 3 character. Tomb diameter is only one metric, however, and certain passage tombs though with smaller diameters can possess sophisticated features equivalent to those found in the Boyne Valley.

Nevertheless, it remains unlikely that there were more than fifteen passage tombs nationally that could be placed this group. It is difficult to provide accurate figures, unfortunately, as several of the largest and most sophisticated cairns remain unopened. This, as noted earlier, has resulted in the confusing situation whereby monuments such as Heapstown Cairn and Queen Maeve's tomb, though almost certainly passage tomb tradition sites are still classed as 'cairns' or 'kerbed cairns' by the Archaeological Survey of Ireland. The sheer size of many of the focal monuments outside the Boyne Valley could indicate they fall into this category, but because they have never been opened it is impossible to discuss their levels of internal sophistication, design features, alignment or the artefacts that are presumably inside (Fig. 6.4). Queen Maeve's tomb, Carns Hill East and West, Heapstown Cairn, all in County Sligo, Carn Dáithí (Ballinrobe) and Eochy's Cairn

Figure 6.4. Queen Maeve's tomb (photograph: author).

(Neale), Co. Mayo and Derrynahinch, Co. Kilkenny might all belong to this category, but without excavation we cannot be certain. Little is known about the impressive cairn at Knockma, Co. Galway but it is a likely passage tomb and warrants further investigation.

Some monuments have been so badly destroyed that they cannot be definitively categorised. A cairn at Donaghanie, Co. Tyrone, was reported to be, "70 yards in circumference" but the site unfortunately now only survives in Sir William Wilde's 1857 account. If Wilde's measurements are correct this monument may have been larger than Queen Maeve's tomb or Heapstown Cairn. Notably, his record indicates the existence of, "numerous sepulchral cells" and vertical stones, "covered with carving, cut into the flag, consisting of volutes, circles, spires, and zig-zag characters" which he compared with those from the Boyne Valley.[19]

Equally, the sophistication of a passage tomb like Knockroe, Co. Kilkenny would not have been fully apparent without a dedicated excavation campaign.[20] Knockroe had a probable quartz façade, and a platform extending out from the tomb. Despite its ruinous condition, this site apparently had two astronomically orientations; both on the winter solstice, one to the rising sun and one to the setting sun. Additionally, it was located near a river and easily accessible. It is also notable for having a considerable amount of passage tomb art, with thirty decorated stones currently identified. Significantly, several of those decorated stones are kerbstones. The sophistication of this small site, only 20 metres in diameter, was such that it spurred the excavation director to detail the surprising amount of comparisons between Knockroe and the main mound at Knowth.[21] There may be other sites that, like Knockroe, do not have a large cairn diameter or volume, but that have features indicating a level of sophistication commensurate with late phase ritual, or that fulfilled that role in the their local context.

The dates from the Mound of the Hostages demonstrate it was constructed at a similar time to Newgrange and Knowth.[22] In scale it seems to be a Type 2 site, but has other features which indicate it was, or ultimately became, somewhere of intense public focus. The centrality of the Hill of Tara in the Meath landscape may be of some significance in this regard (people who know this landscape well use the Hill of Tara as a positional bearing when navigating around this region). As noted previously, the cursus monument is aligned directly on the passage tomb. Whittle has speculated that structures, which may originally have served a primarily religious function could be then laid claim to by particular groups or lineages towards the end of the main phase of their use, and that, "in some sequences particular social groupings annexed this cult for their own purposes, changing shrines into lineage or other ossuaries".[23] The great quantities of human bone from the Mound of the Hostages, from both the Neolithic and Bronze Age, suggest that it may have had importance in this regard, perhaps for especially powerful lineages.[24]

The enormous Cairn D at Loughcrew, 55 m in diameter, must unfortunately remain a mystery, for although an attempt was made to excavate the site, a passage and chamber were never found.[25] It may be a cenotaph (tomb without a burial) as its excavator Conwell thought. Perhaps Cairn D was an attempt to imitate the splendour and sophistication of Newgrange but without the internal sophistication to match its dimensions. It is possible that when Newgrange, Knowth and Dowth were built that regional groups associated with other complexes attempted to match the scale of achievement in the Boyne Valley. Even if the resulting monuments failed to exhibit the same levels of internal sophistication, they could still create cairns of near equivalent dimensions. Cairns L and T were also important focal monuments within the Loughcrew complex and share some features with Boyne Valley but not to the same degree. As discussed in the next chapter they may be examples of focal monuments of slightly earlier date than Newgrange. It is also possible that later phase passage tomb features were added in a *post hoc* manner to certain monuments.

Baltinglass Hill passage tomb is another candidate for this final category of passage tomb. It possesses a flattened façade, contains three separate chambers, had two stone basins (one exceptionally large), three examples of kerbstone art (remarkably rare outside the Boyne Valley), and significant quantities of quartz found inside and outside the monument.[26] The site shares many similarities with the large Boyne Valley passage tombs, which would suggest contemporaneity; however, Early Neolithic dates on cremated human bone point towards a much longer history.[27] The ground-plan of the site suggests it has been remodelled or expanded at least once in its history. The presence of three possible passage tombs within its cairn also may an indication of multiple phases of activity. Notably, one of the carvings is an example of hidden art, potentially indicating the reuse of older stones (see Chapter Seven).[28]

Carrowkeel Cairn F, though collapsed and inaccessible since Macalister's hurried excavation in 1911, appears to have been the preeminent site of the upland clusters. It is the largest and most sophisticated of the excavated monuments on higher ground, and had the most monumental entrance of all the opened sites in the complex. It had a complex chamber with a five-recess design. Notably, a 1.5 m high standing stone was located within its chamber. An internal standing stone is also found at Loughcrew, Cairn L and this could be an indication that these two monuments were constructed at a similar time. Also of interest is that Cairn E nearby has a court at one end which faces back towards Cairn F, perhaps hinting at ceremonial activity in the zone between the two sites. Cairn F may have been focal monument of the complex during the primary use period of the complex. The most sizeable site by far in the Carrowkeel complex, however, is Heapstown Cairn. If Cairn F was the focal monument at Carrowkeel for its earlier use-period, Heapstown may have taken over that role in the latter stages of the complexes development.

Though unexcavated, the enormous cairn at Heapstown, Co. Sligo has features that indicate that it may be in the Type 3 category (Fig. 6.5). It is in the lowlands and hence more accessible than the main groups of sites in the complex, perhaps a concession to the public. In fact, it lies very near the River Unshin, which enters the sea at Ballysadare Bay on the south side of Knocknarea and Carrowmore on the Cúil Irra peninsula, and additionally, via Lough Arrow, it is connected to the Shannon river system. It is exceptionally large, approximately 30,000 cubic tonnes in its original volume and 57 m in diameter. Although it has never been opened, it is probable that there is chamber inside the cairn. Significantly, Heapstown has the only example of kerbstone art from Carrowkeel (a third piece of art within the wider complex).[29] Other features of note include kerbstones that gradually increase in size, highlighting an entrance to the monument, and an external pillar stone (now fallen) perhaps somewhat similar to the example from Knowth West. This conglomeration of late phase features argue that Heapstown Cairn acted as a temple-like site for public ritual within the wider Carrowkeel complex. The construction of Heapstown could be seen as exemplary of what was happening in the passage tomb tradition at this time. It is clearly associated with the passage tombs above and around it in the higher ground, but the community leaders chose to situate their largest construction in a more accessible location, and with a range of features related to public ceremony.

Queen Maeve's tomb serves as the focal point for the Cúil Irra

*Figure 6.5. Heapstown Cairn (drawing by W. F. Wakeman, 1878.
By permission of Sligo County Library).*

region. Its location on the hilltop of Knocknarea lends it tremendous visibility in the surrounding landscape. Harbison eloquently describes it as, "one of the unforgettable reminiscences of the Stone Age vision".[30] Its enormous size and location ensure it has a kind of 'ever-presence' or visual accessibility.[31] Queen Maeve's tomb is noteworthy for having a number of stone settings, mainly around the southern part of its extensive perimeter. Though unexcavated, these settings provide a rare comparison with those at Newgrange and Knowth and perhaps hint at an entrance in this area.[32]

What we begin to see late in the Irish passage tomb tradition is a progression towards temple-like centres, what O'Kelly called "the cathedrals of the megalithic religion".[33] Usually, these monuments occur in the midst of or in association with already existing passage tomb centres. Type 3 monuments indicate a change in the way passage tombs are used: energy was invested into sophisticated sites that were relatively accessible in the landscape and designed for public view. As the largest sites were constructed and used, the focus changed from one with religious rites taking place away from the wider community towards one where public spectacle and ceremony were in the ascendant.

Interpreting change

As previously noted, after 3600 BC the climate in Ireland began to deteriorate. Tellingly, by 3400 BC the forests began to recover across the island. Settlement evidence is scant in this period and wild foods such as berries and nuts show up to a greater extent in the archaeological record.[34] Communities may have needed to make more use of wild resources and perhaps lead a more mobile lifestyle than was previously the case. Though broad changes in the climate affected the whole island, there was regional variation too. Susann Stolze who has examined solar activity and its relationship with climate has suggested that north-west was more negatively affected by the downturn in climate than other parts of Ireland.[35] This may have significance as regards the sequence of passage tomb construction.

Cereal crops were especially vulnerable to extreme weather conditions, potentially making that form of farming unsustainable. Bad harvests may have been especially common in the western part of the country, where soils tended to be lighter and less fertile. As work at Newgrange was underway, human activity in the north-west of Ireland – near the Carrowmore and Carrowkeel passage tomb complexes – had dramatically reduced. Indeed, a complete recovery of the forest in County Sligo had taken place in the last third of the fourth millennium BC.[36] Stolze maintains that, in the east, conditions began to improve in the last quarter of the fourth millennium BC, and notes that, "The timing of the warmer and drier period after 3250 BC overlaps with passage grave construction in the eastern part of the island including the Boyne Valley".[37] This begs the question, had passage tomb construction completely stopped in the north-west of Ireland during that period, with the eastern part of the country (where conditions were marginally better) becoming the primary centre of passage tomb innovation?

Given these changes in climate, it should come as no surprise the greatest amount of activity in the passage tomb tradition seems to have been in the east of Ireland (and perhaps in Wales also) in this period. Though Carrowmore (and Carrowkeel) were certainly still receiving deposits of cremated bone after 3200 BC, evidence for new construction is minimal. In this period, Carrowmore may have been a 'legacy complex', its main phase of construction long over as building at Newgrange was underway. The dynamism of the passage tomb tradition seems to have drifted eastwards.

How are we to characterise these developments? What begins to be observed late in the Irish passage tomb tradition is an ambition to construct monuments that could fulfil more temple-like functions. A tradition that had once been primarily isolationist had increasingly taken a more central and manifestly public role. People had taken centre stage.

Crowdsourcing in the Boyne Valley

In previous accounts, the increasing size and sophistication of passage tombs have been explained through 'competitive construction', rival groups attempting to out-do each other in their building efforts.[38] There may be an element of truth in this; however, the evidence presented here suggests that the various developments which occurred in the passage tomb tradition were primarily the result of changes in ritual emphases over time. Ruling elites may ultimately have taken advantage of these changes, but the primary dynamic was centuries old at that point.

Type 3 sites such as Newgrange indicate a major shift in how passage tombs were thought of and used; energy was invested in creating sophisticated monuments, accessible in the landscape, and designed for public view. The public aspect of the monuments began to assume far greater importance. The implication of the additional features found at passage tombs is that in the last quarter of the fourth millennium BC the monuments and the rituals associated with them were evolving in a way that reflected their importance to a viewing public. Indeed, it is possible the increasing numbers of people involved may have been a factor which of itself changed forms of religious expression.

The movement of the materials for the construction of Newgrange would have necessitated the involvement of a great many people. Presumably, it also required some form of centralised authority to direct what would have been quite complex organisation; essentially large-scale project management. Large groups would also likely have been present to participate in ceremonial events. The greater number of people required to construct ever larger monuments and participate in ceremonies, could have had a kind of democratising effect. One of the reasons why the Brú na Bóinne complex became so important in this later stage of passage tomb construction may have been its relative accessibility (rather than a complex in more mountainous landscape, for instance).

The distance from which materials for the construction of Newgrange were brought hints at a polity with a long reach, potentially extending over much of the modern day province of Leinster, from County Wicklow in the south to County Louth in the north. Indeed, Brady's raw material acquisition study suggests not only routine lithic collection of stone from nearby coasts, but to the importation of chalk flint from County Antrim.[39]

The evidence seems to suggest that some form of centralised power, associated with passage tombs, was growing over the latter third of the fourth millennium BC. If it is supposed, that the political region around the Brú na Bóinne complex was as large as the area from which materials to build Newgrange came, then relatively sophisticated governance may have been necessary. Shannon Fraser has proposed that validation of authority claims may have become an important concern as the largest passage tombs were built at Loughcrew.[40] Equally, in the Boyne Valley, gatherings of a significant portion of the population may have had to be present to assent to a potential leaders claim to power, for it to be considered valid. Though a large population would presumably have been present in the Boyne Valley, if laws or important announcements were promulgated at this time it would make sense that as much of the whole region's population as possible was gathered together to ensure the information became widely known. Large-scale construction projects such as the building of Newgrange could have cemented alliances, diffused conflicts, or perhaps even averted potential uprisings. Opportunities to unify disparate groups may have come through the transportation of building materials, through the construction itself, and through ceremonial seasonal gatherings at the monument.

Thus, sizeable gatherings would have been necessary not only for the construction of the monuments, but for the success of the ceremonies that took place at them, and the successful rule of the authority that oversaw them. So what were the means by which crowds were motivated? What was the relationship between the ruling parties and the people who did the work or attended the ceremonies? These are difficult questions. Though powerful rulers could persuade communities of the need to build a new monument, it is less probable that those groups could be sufficiently controlled to make them attend ceremonies, or undertake seasonal pilgrimage to events. Chris Scarre has noted, "Beliefs, like ritual or esoteric knowledge, are of course a source of power in human societies; they may be manipulated for advantage by individuals or groups. They are not, however, invented merely to mislead and subjugate others".[41] Archaeological over-emphasis on elites can be problematic in many ways, not least because this approach involves the positing of 'bounded individuals' as always pitted against their surrounding society. Is this concept of the individual universally justified by anthropological studies? As Joanna Brück has observed:

> Many societies possess a sociocentric or relational model of the person that constructs the self in terms of interpersonal relationships rather than in terms of the essential characteristics of a bounded individual. This means that those who exercise power are themselves subject to the demands of others. Agency is not an intrinsic attribute of the bounded individual but a product of the network of social relationships that constitute the person.[42]

Groups may have been invested in Newgrange for their own reasons. For instance, they may have been motivated by concerns over a worsening climate; perhaps a communal desire to try and ameliorate increasingly poor harvests. There may also have been a religious euphoria associated with the construction; people would have realised they were part of something exceptional, that they were erecting the greatest monuments ever seen. Alan Barnard and James Woodburn once noted that work transforms 'things' into 'property'.[43] If this is true, then the transformation of materials for the construction of Newgrange must have represented a massive statement of ownership by those involved. That level of involvement suggests that the wider community had a far greater sense of ownership than has been previously considered; certainly more involvement than was necessary for earlier simpler passage tombs. They were giving of themselves, collecting or quarrying and then transforming materials from their (potentially distant) locality for a stake in the monument and the public ceremony from which they would ultimately be beneficiaries. Individuals involved in the construction of Newgrange would probably have felt a certain attachment to the monument. Most families in the area probably had members working on Newgrange, or could point to aspects of the work to which they contributed. Feelings of solidarity and accomplishment would have accompanied these communal efforts, and perhaps celebrations for what had been achieved on behalf of their gods and their community. Eogan's sentiment about Knowth could equally be applied to Newgrange and indeed other Type 3 sites:

> A splendid and infinitely great monument like this was probably intended as more than just a tribute to the dead. It could have been a receptacle or treasury for the emotions, feelings, and thoughts of the clan, while its building was perhaps an act of faith in the future and in the continuation or prolongation of the society.[44]

Doctrinal religiosity at Newgrange?

The Irish passage tomb tradition was sufficiently long-lived and dynamic to allow major turning points in forms of religiosity to be discerned. Previously it was noted that features associated with Type 2 passage tombs were indicative of an 'imagistic' mode of religiosity. The monuments and their locations seemed to reflect distance from the wider public body. They could have been constructed by relatively small groups of people. Art was typically found inside the monuments, pointing to rituals inside the monuments. There was a lack of features intended for external public consumption; only small groups could engage with the monuments interiors. Recesses were suitable places for individuals to sit or perhaps remain for extended periods.

Conversely, doctrinal religiosity is concerned with a priesthood, repetitive ritual and public ceremony.[45] At Newgrange and Knowth, unlike at earlier stages in the passage tomb tradition, specialised religious equipment was present, and presumably specialists who used that equipment. The quality of construction and art implies that skilled artisans were also present. Seasonally repeated ritual took place, and presumably sizeable crowds attended those ceremonies and events. Art was not only found inside the monument, but outside as well, for public view. Recesses, which were formerly open and available for human occupation (and potentially for imagistic rites), were now taken up in some instances with exceptionally large basins. Is it possible that activities at Newgrange and Brú na Bóinne were beginning to assume, or at least approach, a doctrinal mode of religiosity?

Whitehouse originally considered the doctrinal mode as occurring in tandem with literacy (as indicated in the term doctrinal).[46] It would be unsurprising if writing were a critical factor because documentation allows rituals to be codified, to remain steady and unchanging. This in turn allowed for the successful and faithful transmission of religious ideas. Yet subsequent studies have highlighted that writing may not always be necessary for a doctrinal mode of religiosity. The repetitive house building and ceremonies at Çatal Höyük, for instance, have been claimed as an instance where doctrinal patterns are evident.[47] At Çatal

Höyük the evidence suggests, "a shift from esoteric mystery cult to something more ideologically uniform".[48] Could a similar progression have occurred in the passage tomb tradition and at Brú na Bóinne?

Unlike imagistic mode of religiosity, which is concerned with low frequency, emotionally arousing rituals that bind together small groups of participants, the doctrinal mode is concerned with higher frequency, less emotionally intense rituals, applicable to larger, anonymous, and diffusely integrated communities (see Table 3.1). The relative anonymity of groups (to each other) at Newgrange must have been a significant factor if people were coming to the site from significant distances. Well-orchestrated, large group-celebration is apparent, rather than the type of personally intense experiences that are central to the imagistic mode.

The evidence is too limited to allow us to perceive the frequency of the rituals at Newgrange. It may be notable, however, that an interest in the astronomical orientation of passage tombs seems to increase over the period passage tombs were constructed. The calendar year has an obvious rhythm, punctuated by the solar and lunar cycles and seasonal agricultural tasks. In previous chapters, the natural rhythms at Newgrange were discussed, in particular, the yearly round of the sun and the rhythms of the animal world, including the arrival and disappearance of winter birds, migratory fish and other creatures. These rhythms may have provided a kind of template or foundation on which rituals and ceremonies were overlain, and therefore effectively routinized. As Cooney has noted, "Given the importance of seasonal changes in the landscape in terms of light, warmth and resources it would not be surprising if religious ideology became grounded in the landscape and these seasonal changes".[49] Hints of repetitive ritual can be inferred in the dedicated recording of important junctures in the solar year. If groups were celebrating the days or weeks around the equinoxes or seasonal cusps as well as the summer and winter solstices, then several ceremonial periods can be inferred. Allowing time for groups to travel to Newgrange (or the most significant site in their region), and several days for the celebration proper, the whole event may have taken a week or two. If other festivals took as long, then four or eight weeks of the year could potentially have been dedicated to ritualised events and ceremonies.

The doctrinal mode has been described as, "always delicately balanced between the competing demands of popular consent and priestly control".[50] The exploration of crowd mobilisation at Newgrange discussed in the previous section seems to point to a similar balance. A centralised authority would have been necessary for the gathering of materials and construction work to be accomplished, yet a certain amount of willing cooperation and community 'buy-in' must have been present for the project to be a success. Not only is the doctrinal mode an indicator of centralised power, it actually encourages centralisation and hierarchical institutions.[51] Interestingly, Whitehouse *et al.* believe:

> The earliest functions of religion were not to legitimate political or economic inequalities. Initially religion's function was to bind together small tribal groups, but gradually, as agriculture intensified, this ancient function faded and religion became a means of producing much larger (if more diffuse) group identities.[52]

Such a description could easily be applied to the developments across the passage tomb tradition described in this book.

The scale of Newgrange suggests that the communities or the authority which led them were increasingly successful. This level of ambition is unmatched in Neolithic Ireland. Another feature of the doctrinal mode is its ability to spread quickly.[53] The apparent wealth of Newgrange and the Boyne complex and the influence of passage tomb developments at Brú na Bóinne in other regions would seem to suggest that this society was very successful, and that its reach extended quite far. Connections with northern Britain, seem to be apparent from at least 2900 BC.[54] Some of the objects and art from Brú na Bóinne also hint at connections with even more distant regions, especially Iberia.[55] It is difficult to think of any of the other major passage tomb complexes as this successful and connected. The achievements at Brú na Bóinne must have been founded on a very stable political and religious foundation.

CHAPTER SEVEN

A Secret History

A carver raises the chisel and strikes; the old symbols are stubborn, take time to remove. But the stones will have a new life. They will be needed for this new wonder – a temple to shine forth to all the world.

Megalithic art is perhaps one of the most interesting and yet one of the most difficult features of passage tomb design. Elsewhere I have written about the diverse interpretations of passage tomb art.[1] One problem with previous interpretation is that there is a tendency for explanations and interpretations to be unifactoral. This approach may be unsuitable for the variety of art that exists in the passage tomb tradition and the length of time over which it evolved. We would not consider explaining several hundred years of twentieth century art with one theory or idea.

At Newgrange, some carvings are sophisticated and accomplished in appearance. Others appear elementary or haphazard, sufficiently so to have been described as 'doodles' or 'graffiti'.[2] It has been a source of puzzlement that haphazard and rudimentary designs can be found at monuments which also feature art of the most labour intensive and sophisticated kind. The contradiction lessens somewhat when the time-depth of the art is factored in, as attempted in this chapter. A chronological perspective of the art also provides fascinating clues to the history of Newgrange. As noted previously, one can observe that carvings are sometimes superimposed upon earlier designs, suggesting a kind of artistic stratigraphy. It is only at Brú na Bóinne that ample evidence of all the main styles of passage tomb art exist and this is why Newgrange and Knowth in particular are so useful for investigating the evolution of art-making in the passage tomb tradition.

Hidden art

One of the most intriguing aspects of design at Newgrange is the phenomenon of hidden art. Hidden art, as the name suggests, was placed in a position not visible to someone circling or entering the final construction. Art can be obscured in several ways. Most frequently, it is placed in a position impossible to view: on the side of a kerbstone which faces into the cairn or on the underside the kerb; on the upper-side of a passage lintel or chamber roofstone; on the portion of an orthostat beneath ground level; or on a stone, or part of a stone, within the body of the cairn. Alternatively, it can be partially or completely obscured by adjacent construction stones. Finally, some art could be hidden because of the superimposition of later art, even though faint traces may still survive.

An examination of classic passage tomb motifs (*e.g.* spirals, lozenges, chevrons), has shown that hidden art comprises approximately 18% of the total corpus in Ireland.[3] Many examples of hidden art probably remain unrecorded at monuments which have not been excavated. Even at extensively excavated sites like Newgrange and Knowth, art may still remain hidden. The lower parts of twenty-six of the ninety seven kerbstones at Newgrange (K21–K47) have not been uncovered and it is probable that further hidden art would be revealed if the inner faces of those stones were exposed.

Kerbstones K13 and K18 bear the best known examples of this phenomenon at Newgrange. They are the most profusely decorated, each having over one hundred individual motifs (Fig. 7.1). Hidden art was also uncovered on K4 and K11 during the O'Kelly-led excavations. The art on each of these four kerbstones faces directly into the cairn and consequently could only have been revealed through excavation. Further hidden carvings were revealed in the 1980s when kerbstones K56–79 at the rear of Newgrange were uncovered in excavations directed by Ann Lynch.[4] As well as the long-documented carving on

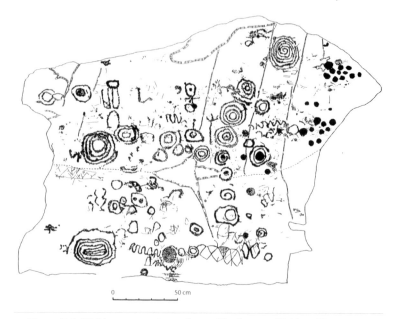

Figure 7.1. Hidden art on inner face of kerbstone (K13) at Newgrange (after C. O'Kelly 1982, fig. 26).

K67, additional carvings were found on nine kerbstones. Five of these kerbstones had art on hidden surfaces (K56, K58, K61, K66 and K76). Two stones had art on their upper surfaces (K73 and K76), which may also have been hidden depending on the original form of the cairn. It is striking that of the kerbs with art (whether on the front of the backs of stones) approximately one quarter of it was hidden.

As well as on kerbstones, hidden art is also found inside Newgrange in the passage and chamber. It is clear that the passage orthostats R3, L19 and L20 were carved previous to their erection because in each case they have art on the portion of the stone within the ground (*i.e.*, the carvings could not have been made once the stones were in position) (Fig. 7.2). Two other passage stones, L13 and R12, have art on their side faces which is obscured by adjacent stones, and hence they had to be carved before the neighbouring stones were in position.

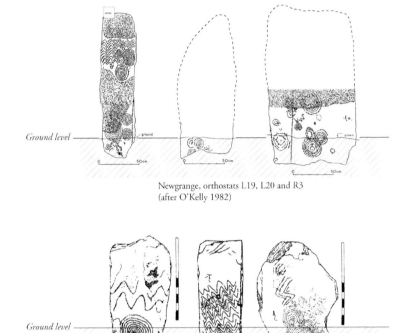

Newgrange, orthostats L19, L20 and R3
(after O'Kelly 1982)

Knowth West, orthostats 18, 74 and 81
(Eogan 1998)

Figure 7.2. Orthostats from Newgrange and Knowth with art occurring beneath ground level (illustration: Guillaume Robin 2009, fig. 186).

An additional nine stones with examples of hidden art were found above the passage when the outer part of the passage was dismantled in the course of excavations, some of it on the upper side of roofstones.[5] The back corbel of the roof-box was profusely decorated (Plate 8, upper). Cumulatively, there are at least fifty motifs in this area that would never have been visible once the construction was complete.

The chamber was not dismantled during excavations so it is not known what additional hidden art may be there. However, in the nineteenth century both Samuel Fergusson and George Coffey had observed hidden art in the chamber at Newgrange.[6] At that time, the famous three-spiral stone, C10, leaned outwards and art could be seen on the stones that lay behind it. Whether some older construction stones simply remained in their former positions as the chamber was rebuilt is a question that cannot be answered at present; however, the art behind C10 raises the possibility of more hidden art behind other chamber stones. It is also notable that designs found on some of the corbel stones within the chamber, such as Co.2/C.14 and Co.1/C.7, sometimes continue into the cairn, and again must have been carved before being placed in position (see below).[7] Conspicuously, this piece is located at the back of the east recess immediately beneath the heavily decorated and probably reused roofstone. Perhaps both ill-fitting stones have originated in the same older monument.

Seemingly, at Newgrange, hidden art was found on the kerbstones, on the passage orthostats and roofstones, among the chamber orthostats and corbels – in fact in just about every part of the monument. What could explain this phenomenon; why was so much of the art from Newgrange hidden?

Why hide art?

The phenomenon of hidden art has been noted for over a hundred and fifty years, and various explanations have been forthcoming. One explanation is that the art could have been created for reasons that were primarily symbolic.[8] Perhaps the visibility of the art may have been less important than the act of carving? This might be so if the art was intended for the dead or for deities, rather than for human eye. However, art was not only obscured by hiding, but was also intentionally removed using pick-dressing. As more than one technique has been used to remove the art from visibility, one must assume that its removal was indeed the primary aim rather than symbolic aspirations.

Alternatively, there are practical explanations why art might be hidden. For instance, it could simply be evidence of changes to the design plan of the monument which occurred during the process of construction, as M. J. O'Kelly and others have suggested.[9] Another functional explanation is that hidden art may be evidence of artists/carvers of varying grades of expertise: the practice works of the less accomplished carvers intentionally concealed in the final construction.[10] Though both of these are plausible explanations, and certainly could explain some pieces, neither quite accounts for the quantities of hidden art known to exist. The answer must be more fundamental.

Another possibility is simply that hidden art may have been older than the monument. Sir William Wilde came to this conclusion in 1849:

> The following very remarkable circumstance struck us while investigating this ancient structure of New Grange, some years ago. We found that those carvings not only covered portions of the stones exposed to view, but extended over those surfaces which, until some recent dilapidation, were completely concealed from view, and where a tool could not have reached them; and the inference is plain, that these stones were carved prior to their being placed in their present position; perhaps were used for some anterior purpose. If so, how much it adds to their antiquity![11]

If the stones were older, then how much older were they; could they even be requisitioned from a now defunct monument or monuments?[12] In the 1960s and 1970s when the O'Kelly's were working at Newgrange, there was less awareness that monuments at Brú na Bóinne, and megalithic sites generally, were sometimes built using materials from older monuments. Eogan's 1998 paper *Knowth before Knowth,* which proposed that older materials were used in the construction of Knowth, was one of the first to properly discuss this aspect of a Brú na Bóinne passage tomb. If hidden art is more ancient, if recycled from older monuments, it raises the possibility that some of it may have been intentionally hidden because in form or style was no longer relevant or desirable? Significantly, O'Sullivan has noted that at Knowth art of standardised character is exclusively on the back of kerbstones but when on the front face it is superimposed by new styles of art, *i.e.*, older forms of art were more likely to be hidden.[13]

Evidence of recycled stones is not only apparent with the hidden art at Newgrange, but also through some of the visible art. Claire O'Kelly noted that at Newgrange the lintel of the roof-box and the lintels and decorated corbels in the chamber did not quite fit the position for which they were used and concluded from this that they were carved on the ground before being placed in position.[14] Inaccuracies would only have become apparent when the stone was in position. However, rather than being carved on the ground, it seems more likely they were originally carved a long time before Newgrange was built. The fact that the art did not quite fit its position, or was not fully displayed, may not be because the carvers were unable to get their measurements right; rather it could signify that it had originated in an earlier monument (where it fit accurately).

The wonderful piece of art that now acts as a ceiling over the right recess is a good example of a carving that is likely to have been taken from elsewhere (Fig. 7.3). This can be inferred because much of the design is not seen; the work was simply too large for the position it which it was placed. As a consequence, portions of its design are completely occluded by the recess orthostats or buried within the cairn at the side and back of the recess. Unlike the hidden kerbstone art in which the designs often appear random and haphazard, this is a much more composed-looking piece. This is significant; its re-use implies not all older artworks were thought undesirable by the builders – some were still deemed worthy of display.

Art history

Awareness of the quantities of hidden art at Newgrange allow us to see the site and its art differently. The monument has preserved not only art created when the stones were in position, but art from

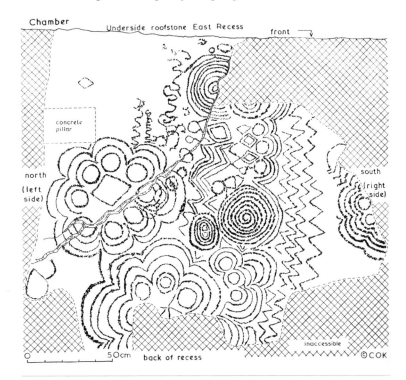

Figure 7.3. East recess roofstone art, Co.2/14, Newgrange. Note areas of occluded art (after C. O'Kelly 1982, fig. 51).

earlier periods as well. Indeed, bar a few select pieces, it is a distinct possibility that the majority of the stones with artwork at Newgrange were recycled from earlier passage tombs. The monument could be considered an artistic 'time capsule'. Might it be possible to go further, perhaps to identify a spectrum of art which Neolithic communities deemed more or less suitable for display? Such a gauge would be valuable as it could permit a glimpse into the decision-making of those responsible for the monument.

If many of the art-covered stones were recycled from older sites, arguably the most 'authentic' Newgrange art, *i.e.*, the art that most

Figure 7.4. Newgrange entrance stone, K1. Note undecorated base uncovered during excavations (photograph: M. J. O'Kelly).

reflects the preferences of the communities that built the monument, are those pieces which were carved *in situ*. These are the pieces that we know were not taken from earlier structures but instead reflected the preferences of the communities as Newgrange was constructed. This art includes K1, K52 which may have been specially created. Possibly K67 and the decorated lintel above the roof-box could also fall into this category. One could call these commissioned pieces.

The entrance stone, K1, is particularly interesting. Clearly, it was carved *in situ* because the carving stops where the stone meets ground level (Fig. 7.4). Yet, because the carvings flow around the edges of the stone, the work had to be done before neighbouring kerbstones, K2 and K97, were placed either side of it (unless those weighty kerbs were temporally moved). The stone may have been carefully chosen for the all-important entrance position before it was covered in designs and then carved *in situ*. One can imagine the master artist working as other construction activities were taking place around him or her, and perhaps desperately trying to avoid a serious mistake. Knowing the stone was already secure in its final position, there could be no second chances.

Pick-dressing can also provide useful information about the phasing of the carvings, and insights into the art that was considered most important as Newgrange was underway. Most pick-dressing seems to have been completed when the construction stones were already in position. On many of the orthostats it does not continue below ground level, and often to around 20 cm above the current floor level (this level may be an indication of the height of the original floor).[15] Though the date of the technique is uncertain, it seems to supersede all other art at Newgrange, even covering stones with art carved *in situ,* such as the entrance stone. But how much later did pick-dressing occur? Was it applied by a later group, perhaps in an iconoclastic removal of images created by leaders at Newgrange?[16] Or did pick-dressing represent just another aspect of the original artists' creative repertoire?

Claire O'Kelly argued for the contemporaneity of pick-dressing with Newgrange's construction.[17] She noted that the technique was not always used to remove earlier artwork but in fact was often used to enhance existing pieces. For example, on stone L19 the person applying the pick-dressing went to great care to remove all the material around the artwork, respectfully following the curved edge of the carving without ever running over it (Plate 4). Notably, the pick-dressing method had an aesthetic value as well, removing imperfections in the stone and bringing out its colour.[18] The value of the technique can be seen when contrasting the stones at Dowth with those at Newgrange. At Dowth, the technique is much less in evidence, and even the internal stones there look rougher and more weathered than at Newgrange, where all the passage stones and many of the chamber stones have pick-dressing.[19] O'Kelly also highlighted that pick-dressing even occurs on corbels within the chamber. This indicates that the technique was thought of as a positive contribution to the stone in and of itself; its application was not only for the purpose of removing unwanted art but had other roles too.

Given the strong possibility that materials at Newgrange and Knowth may have originated in earlier monuments, one of the reasons pick-dressing came to be used may have been in response to a situation where weathered stones with older art needed to be renewed for reuse. Pick-dressing would have been a means to give old construction stones new life. Only the best, most relevant, art would be kept. Undesirable or out-of-fashion motifs could be erased through the technique, with the added benefit that the freshness of the stone and its colour would be renewed by removing a layer of material. Many of the stones at Newgrange are of greywacke that, contrary to its name, has an attractive green hue. The colouring of the stone would have been enhanced by pick-dressing.

Some instances of older art unsuitable for display could be more easily hidden by facing them into the cairn. By not requiring labour-intensive pick-dressing, this solution would represent a good labour-saving. Notably, on several orthostats at Newgrange and Knowth, art appears on parts of the stones beneath ground level; again, in these instances it was not necessary to use pick-dressing to remove the art, as it could easily be hidden. If removing motifs was the primary role of pick-dressing, it raises questions as to whether this was passage tomb 'art', and whether it should be included in totals of stones with passage tomb art in Ireland.[20]

After works made *in situ,* the second most valued group of designs at Newgrange may be the carvings on recycled stones which were retained in their entirety for display, even though they could have been hidden. In these cases, someone decided that the pieces were sufficiently in tune with the current preferences and requirements that they should be displayed, even though they were of older vintage. This is so with regard to the fine piece over the eastern recess already mentioned (Fig. 7.3). Though the stone and its art are likely to be from an earlier monument, the piece has been deemed sufficiently important to feature in one of the most ritually potent parts of the new monument, the favoured right-hand recess (see Chapter Two). I think it can be concluded in this instance that the design must still have held considerable meaning for these communities.

The next most prioritised art may be motifs on a reused stone which were left intact and displayed, even as other motifs on the same stone were intentionally removed by pick-dressing. This is very apparent on stone L19 where some motifs were almost completely removed using pick-dressing, yet other motifs or compositions were left untouched (Plate 4). Notably, on the portion of the stone in the ground, art occurs again (Fig. 7.2); presumably this was because it was more convenient for the art to be hidden within the earth than to chisel it away.

The seemingly haphazard removal of art puzzled Claire O'Kelly.[21] Why were some motifs obliterated by pick-dressing yet others designs left unscathed? If the stones were from earlier monuments, however, it would be unsurprising that the pick-dressers would consciously select which of the older art pieces should be removed and which could be retained on the basis of current preferences. This lends additional significance to the surviving pieces. They allow us to see which designs were most respected as Newgrange was being constructed and which were no longer considered relevant.

It also raises questions about why certain motifs were deselected: what could those older forms of art represent? What was it about those pieces that led to them being hidden away? Inexpert art could be disguised for aesthetic reasons, but perhaps there were more fundamental considerations also, even political motives. This would be the case if the removed art was the product of religious rituals which were no longer relevant; rituals no longer deemed appropriate for the changed circumstances when Newgrange was built. Could it be that the rituals associated with Type 2 monuments were outmoded or somehow considered inappropriate for the role intended for Newgrange? Had some art become undesirable because it was the product of subjective individual visions, so-called entoptic art?

Whitehouse has observed that strong central authority is rarely a feature of religions in the imagistic mode because peoples' religious experiences are thought to come directly from the gods or ancestors rather than mediated by priests or leaders.[22] Revelation was a bottom-up affair. An examination of the evolution of passage tomb art suggests that when Newgrange was built the past was being actively hidden, its message regulated. Somebody was deciding what art should be most prominent and which should be dismissed. Motifs and symbols which at one point were important in the passage tomb tradition were now removed, hidden or else absorbed into sculptural art pieces reflecting different ideologies.

If developments in passage tomb art are examined across Ireland over the *longue durée,* what becomes apparent is that aesthetic considerations – harmonious composition, visual effect, size of the art – appear to take precedence over time. The tradition of depicting simple motifs, what most people would see as 'classic' passage tomb art, diminishes in importance. The artwork also seems to become much more organised and betrays a sense of planned composition. For instance, the rectangular design at the entrance to Knowth West is repeated on the backstone of the chamber in a way suggesting the implementation of an overall concept through the design. The most sophisticated art style at Newgrange is one that draws on a core group of passage tomb motifs, which may have originated at an earlier stage, but uses them as blocks in building sophisticated compositions. The finest examples are the entrance stone K1, and the kerbstone directly opposite to the rear of Newgrange, K52.

As Claire O'Kelly once noted:

> It seems to me … that the symbolical meaning was the original inspiration for Irish passage-grave art, beginning with the random carving of motifs which had meaning for those that applied them, or who caused them to be applied, and that it was only with the passage of time, as the tomb builders became more expert and sophisticated generally, that the aesthetic element of the carvings began to emerge and develop and designs and patterns began to be achieved, though perhaps this aspect never entirely overruled the symbolism, latent or otherwise.[23]

Hence designs that originally may have been associated with 'symbolic meaning' became absorbed into a repertoire of motifs deemed appropriate for inclusion in planned art pieces. If so, as Newgrange was under construction, passage tomb carvers were employing a culturally sanctioned range of motifs rather than making direct recordings of internal experience. Though the art at Newgrange has been used to discuss the possibility of shamanic or trance ritual, the evidence suggests the opposite; though perception altering rites may have had an important role at one stage of the passage tomb tradition, it was no longer as relevant when Newgrange was under construction. When Claire O'Kelly once described the visible (non-hidden) art at Newgrange as 'official art', she may have put her finger on an important distinction between hidden and visible art: that there was a ruling entity, whether religious or political or both, who decided which art was official, which was correct to display and which was undesirable.[24] Equally, Eogan has noted that:

> Perhaps changing ritual ideas meant that the original meaning of some compositions was no longer relevant, and it became necessary to destroy such compositions so as to conform to current values or at least to reduce the composition's power.[25]

Subjective, unplanned art, or the type of rituals upon which those practices were supported, may no longer have been relevant as Newgrange was constructed – it had a different role.

Past lives

It seems many of the carved stones at Newgrange were reused from earlier monuments. The recycled stones may have been sourced from older monuments in the surrounding landscape or alternatively taken from an earlier monument on the same site, an earlier Newgrange. Even without the art-based evidence discussed above, however, there are several indications that Newgrange had earlier incarnations.

The excavations undertaken by M. J. O'Kelly uncovered a turf mound under the cairn at Newgrange, which he mooted could have covered an older passage tomb or other structure.[26] This mound was confirmed by the subsqent 1980s excavations, but its projected diameter increased to 45–50 m through that work.[27] O'Kelly believed this large internal mound explained the unusual shape of the Newgrange; its southern perimeter bulging outwards to accommodate this turf mound. However, the mound continues outside of the kerbstones, *i.e.*, the kerbs actually cross over rather than simply enclose the turf mound.[28] Very little more is known about this mound; we do not even know whether the monument was entirely composed of turves, or if a stone monument could lie within it as O'Kelly proposed. Though we cannot say it was a passage tomb, given it is surrounded by passage tombs, covered by a passage tomb, and that Sites K and L alongside Newgrange also had it turf covering, it certainly seems possible. At the very least, given its context, it has to be considered a passage tomb tradition monument. If a passage tomb, its size, though less than today's Newgrange, would still make it one of the larger passage tombs in Ireland. Dates retrieved from the turf, and the absence of a layer of humus between the turf mound and the covering cairn, suggest that Newgranges' cairn may have been constructed relatively soon after the turf was laid down.[29] Was the turf placed over an older monument as a way of protecting and sealing a previous passage tomb? Had some of its construction stones been used to build the larger monument above it; perhaps some of its art-covered stones too? Whatever lies beneath it, this substantial mound is the first monument we have knowledge of on this site, and hence can be referred to as Newgrange I.

At some point Newgrange I was covered, and hence at least one other monument can be inferred: a Newgrange II. However, the newer passage tomb cannot be the monument seen today, because there is evidence of at least one intermediary site. During the primary excavations, layers of turf were discovered within the body of the cairn behind the kerbstone 95 (to the right of the entrance). Those turf layers were not part of Newgrange I; rather they appeared to spread through the body of the cairn. Palle Eriksen has proposed that the turf layers recorded by O'Kelly each represent several years of growth, when cairns of smaller size were exposed to the elements.[30] Those turf layers were not present in the more recently excavated area, however, which places a question mark over Eriksen's model.[31]

Nevertheless, at Newgrange other indicators of phases of reconstruction may be present. The passage design is interesting in this regard. It has a slightly snaking form; as one progresses up-slope into the monument, it subtly curves, first to the left, and to the right. At orthostats R10–12/L11–13, halfway between the entrance and the end of the chamber, it begins to straighten again as one advances towards the chamber (Fig. 7.5). This is also the position of the lowest passage lintel. This juncture where the passage appears to buckle could represent the limits of a once shorter passage. Of interest is the natural spring which is found under orthostat R8, on the right-hand side of the passage just before this juncture. It might be considered unusual that the builders would decide to place passage orthostats on top of a spring; but perhaps less so if they were extending a previously existing passage and had no choice but to continue over the spring as the direction of the passage was already fixed.

It may also be significant that the roof-box structure at Newgrange is set 2.5 m back from the entrance, some way back along the passage. Indeed, since the nineteenth century the position of the roof-box together with the fact that the passage entrance was some distance from the outer kerb led Fergusson to conclude that a façade had been added to the monument.[32] These features are not typical of passage tomb construction and may find their best explanation in an episode of remodelling. If remodelling was more focused at the front of the monument, it might explain why O'Kelly found layers of turves within the cairn near the entrance area (those interpreted as phases of rebuilding by Eriksen), but that similar evidence did not seem to occur at the later excavated north-eastern periphery of the mound.[33] Remodelling of the front of the monument would also make sense in a context where increasing emphasis was placed on display and visual impact. It may be notable that O'Kelly recorded a series of boulders within the cairn behind K51–53.[34] These may be inner revetments as O'Kelly believed but the materials could also be from an older site or an older phase at Newgrange. Indeed, the heart-shaped appearance of the mound would be better explained if the front of monument was extended; as its volume would be increased in that area it would naturally lend it a front-heavy appearance when viewed in plan. The greater bulk of the southern half of the cairn, the existence of turves

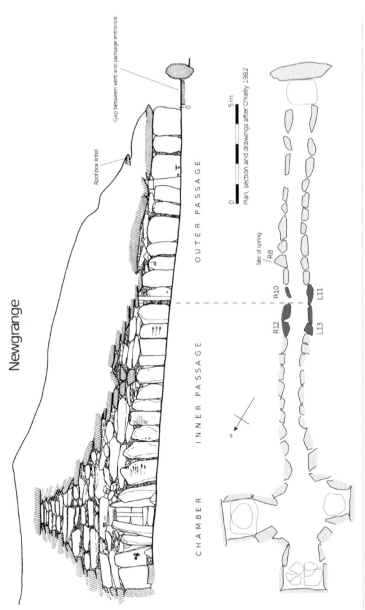

Figure 7.5. Newgrange plan and elevation (after O'Kelly 1982, fig. 4 and Robin 2008, fig. 6.32).

in the body of the cairn especially behind the entrance area, the apparent step-back from the kerb to the passage entrance, the further step-back to the roof-box, together with the possible extension to the passage would all find explanation if (one or more) extensions to the monument were primarily concentrated at the front part of the monument.

Finally, the 1980s excavations have provided evidence that the quartz layer did not surround the monument until the Chalcolithic period, after 2500 BC. The changes which occurred at Newgrange in that period fall outside the scope of this work, yet they do have a bearing on our understanding of how quartz was employed in the construction at Newgrange. The dates returned on a cow's tooth from under the quartz at K79, together with a Chalcolithic period flint core from the same context, indicate the quartz could not have been laid down in the Neolithic period.[35] Moreover, the ground on which the quartz was found had been stripped of vegetation, thus suggesting that the changes were purposeful rather than the result of an unplanned collapse, *i.e.*, that it was intentionally used to create a platform around the monument during a post-Neolithic phase of remodelling.[36] This reworking of the monument may have happened at the same time Newgrange's entrance was sealed, and newer circular features were constructed in the area, in particular the large ceremonial post and pit circle. One wonders was Newgrange sealed just as the turf mound had been previously, was this part of the life cycle of these passage tombs?

It is tempting to refer to this last phase as Newgrange IV. For present purposes, however, the observation of three major phases is sufficient: Newgrange I (turf mound), Newgrange II (evinced by indications of expansion and remodelling of the cairn and the re-use of older materials and art) and Newgrange III (the monument excavated by O'Kelly).[37] One of the implications of these earlier monuments, Newgrange I and II, is that today's Newgrange physically contains earlier passage tomb tradition history. Consequently, not only is Newgrange the result of a process of passage tomb development in Ireland but, like a Russian doll, it literally embodies that earlier history through the earlier monuments from which it is composed.

CHAPTER EIGHT

Journey to Newgrange

For generations praise was heaped upon the ancestors, great temples raised. Yet all things, even wonders of the world, must one-day fade. In the shadow of the Brú new circles are made. We turn to the sky once again.

There are over two hundred passage tombs on this island and taken together they demonstrate a gradual build-up of knowledge within the passage tomb tradition, including at least two decisive changes in the form and role of the monuments. Almost all the component elements at Newgrange – various construction features, the astronomical orientation, the art and design, the artefacts found within its chamber and so on – can be traced back to earlier precursors around Ireland. Newgrange is not one of the first Irish passage tombs built as was once thought; it is in fact one of the late examples, a new kid on the block. The revised chronology at Carrowmore and dates from the similar passage tomb at Broadsands in south-west Britain (and Early Neolithic dates on bone from Baltinglass, Co. Wicklow), suggest that Newgrange appears after approximately half a millennium of previous passage tomb activity on this island. The first passage tombs were coastal monuments with an ancestral focus, and may have been connected to beliefs around physical and metaphysical journeys over the sea. The groups who built those sites may have come from north-west France to Britain and Ireland, or perhaps from north-west France to Britain and then to Ireland. The most likely time for this was approximately 3900–3800 BC, as the passage tomb tradition in Brittany came to an end, and as agriculture was becoming established in these islands.

Around the middle of the fourth millennium BC, larger passage tombs were built at a remove from general society. They were located in restricted landscapes – uplands, or surrounded by water – and often clustered. A new form of creative expression, megalithic art, and a fascination with observing the light of the sun on its journey through the year were two new developments that took place in this period. These new passage tomb centres were important zones of ritual activity and may have been connected with religious training. Over many generations, greater and greater energy was invested into passage tomb construction within these complexes. Increasing aggrandisement of the monuments, rebuilding and enlarging of the most hallowed structures, eventually led to a new type of passage tomb, focal monuments, with a peculiarly public emphasis. Religious rites and leadership roles within these communities may have been deeply entwined in this period; the once isolationist tradition had moved to the very centre of political and social life.

Arrow of time 2

As noted in Chapter One, at various times in the past an east-west or a west-east sequence of development of Irish passage tombs had been in favour. Having reviewed various aspects of the monuments, we are now in a better position to again consider the growth and development of the passage tomb tradition on this island. One may be tempted to conclude that as the monuments at Carrowmore have been shown to be older than Newgrange, and that there appears to be more late passage tomb features and design in the east, that the west-east model of sequential construction is the more accurate model. The situation is more nuanced, however.

An examination of Type 1 passage tombs suggests the earliest phase of passage tomb construction takes place not in the east or west, but both in the east and the west, along the coasts, especially in the northern half of the island. If the Type 1 sites in each region were constructed at approximately the same time is not clear; perhaps the clustered group at Carrowmore are later than the more dispersed examples in Antrim. Similar monuments are also found along the west coast of Britain. This initial seeding was followed by the construction of larger monuments suitable for human entry – Type 2 passage tombs – spread over much of the countryside. Once again they are located primarily in the northern half of the island, though often further inland than the earlier monuments, and found especially on hilltops or places apart. We do not know why passage tombs are predominantly found in the northern part of the island; cultural or religious boundaries may have existed of which we are unaware.

Equally, we do not have enough chronological information to fill in the details of this process of development across the country, but clearly the situation is more complex than a simple uni-directional model. The process may be better characterised as a 'mushrooming' which occurred around a number of passage tomb hubs. The four main complexes had a crucial role, but developments at other significant, though less investigated, clusters such as Kilmonaster in the north-west and Bremore on the east coast may have been important, too. Each of the larger clusters had their own, in some cases, lengthy, internal histories. Eventually, exceptionally large and sophisticated focal sites emerged within or nearby to these influential hubs.

Though a simple west–east sequence of development does not accurately capture developments within the tradition, nevertheless as regards the four major complexes, it is undeniable that later forms of passage tomb, artefacts and megalithic art do occur in the eastern part of the island to a greater extent than in the west. Thus, at least regarding the latter part of the passage tomb tradition in Ireland (3200–2900 BC), it may be fair to conclude that the centre of power and creativity within the tradition gradually drifts eastward. Perhaps a better way to frame this is to say that new constructions and design ideas continued to be implemented at Brú na Bóinne when they had come to a halt in the other major complexes. Similarly, some of the developments at Loughcrew are not replicated to the same extent at Carrowmore or Carrowkeel. A deteriorating climate, which had a greater impact in the west of Ireland, may be one reason late-phase design and construction is not as apparent in the west.

Yet there were periods, particularly in the last third of the fourth millennium BC, where all four major complexes were ritually active places. We know, for instance, that the monuments at Carrowmore and Carrowkeel were still being used to receive deposits of bone at the same time Newgrange was under construction.[1] The difference is that even though deposits of human bone were still being placed in the chambers in the west of Ireland, for instance at Carrowmore, the primary or dominant phase of construction in that complex was probably over.

Nevertheless, some degree of stitching forward and back from east to west may have taken place in this late phase, instances where new developments from the east were incorporated into the western complexes. The construction of Queen Maeve's tomb (which is surrounded by the remains of far simpler passage tombs) and Heapstown Cairn (below an older complex in the uplands), are probably representative of this late-phase activity. The denudation of many of the smaller megalithic sites that surround Queen Maeve's tomb could indicate that material was taken from them to expand the focal monument, perhaps to ensure its status as the pre-eminent monument of the Cúil Irra region. The instances of passage tomb art at three monuments in the north-west (Listoghil, Cairn B, Carrowkeel, Heapstown) could also reflect those influences.

Though the chronological data is admittedly rather limited, the developmental process outlined in this book can be seen through an analysis of the individual complexes.

The major complexes

This section characterises each of four main passage tomb complexes with regard to their position in the developmental sequence outlined in this book. To achieve this, it is first necessary to appreciate factors which obscure those sequences. To begin with, these complexes (and the monuments within them) may have had long and involved use-histories. They are effectively palimpsests: places with many-layered histories. In most instances, it is only the final building phase which is immediately apparent, a snapshot of a monument or a complex in its mature phase. Rarely, for instance, do we have information on the previous monuments that may have stood precisely where the monument under investigation is found, as we now have to some extent at Newgrange and Knowth. Even in circumstances where excavation has taken place, much can still be unknown. It is striking that even though Newgrange has been extensively excavated there is still almost nothing known about the role of the turf mound (or turf-covered structure) which exists within it. It is likely that there were similar periods of expansion and embellishment at Heapstown Cairn and Queen Maeve's tomb which would be revealed if these cairns were to be excavated.

Another problem which makes reading these complexes difficult is that passage tomb complexes or individual monuments could be adapted, re-modified or completely reconstituted in the past, thus making it difficult to assign them to only one passage tomb type. For example, a monument could begin life as modest passage tomb suitable for Type 2 ritual and then later be adapted for public-oriented rites; thus a single monument can straddle different phases. Moreover, several Irish passage tombs may have been 'retro-fitted' for public ritual, probably late in their use history. That is, they have some late features, but in scale or sophistication were not originally constructed as dedicated face-to-the-world public-oriented monuments. It should also be recognised that the largest and most sophisticated passage tombs are not the last passage tombs built in Ireland. At both Newgrange and Knowth, there are indications that some smaller passage tombs were erected after the construction of the main monument.[2]

For all these limitations, it is still possible to use the developmental model outlined here to at least identify the signature phase of activity in each of the four main complexes and perhaps to begin to discern the broad sequence of activities at each location. Thus, what follows is not a detailed account of the history of each complex, but only a broad-stroke examination of each in relation to the approximate sequence of passage tomb construction outlined in this book. More comprehensive reconstructions of the phases of construction at each location can be found elsewhere: for instance, Cooney's study of phases of activity at Brú na Bóinne and Loughcrew; Eogan's works on the main site at Knowth; Fraser's unusual and insightful analysis of developments at Loughcrew; and Stefan Bergh's in-depth analysis of developments at Carrowmore and throughout the Cúil Irra peninsula.[3] As more chronological information becomes available, our understanding of developments within these complexes will inevitably change and improve, and previous accounts will be revised or refined.

Carrowmore

Bar the unusual central site, Carrowmore is almost entirely composed of the simple form Type 1 passage tombs which were discussed in Chapter One. These passage tombs are early in the tradition; most likely to have been built from 3750–3500 BC. The recent radiocarbon dating project, however, indicates that the chambers at Carrowmore were used for the entire period of the passage tomb tradition, even if further passage tombs were no longer constructed within the complex.

Notably, most of the sites are not visible from afar; indeed, they are largely invisible until one is upon them. Several seem to be located away from the highest points in immediate landscape. Carrowmore 7 for instance is constructed on a slope, seemingly intentionally avoiding the higher ground immediately above it (Fig. 8.1). The emphasis seems to be on the view from the sites, rather than the visibility of the sites from a distance (unlike many later passage tombs). Fraser has referred to passage tombs which appear to subtly accentuate pre-existing qualities of place, as 'sympathetic' sites, in contrast with later, usually more substantial monuments that tend to physically dominate the topography, including enforcing new patterns of movement within the landscape.[4] The majority of the Carrowmore sites are of the sympathetic variety.

It is only at the central monument at Carrowmore, Listoghil, which is of very different form and scale than other tombs in the complex, where late features are displayed. The monument is 30 m in

Figure 8.1. Carrowmore 7 with Queen Maeve's tomb in the background (photograph: Ken Williams).

diameter, has remnants of a surrounding platform, and has one stone on which passage tomb art is found.[5] At what point in the Neolithic period art was applied to the monument though is an open question. It is possible that megalithic art was belatedly added to some sites as carved designs became an important part of passage tomb elaboration late in the tradition. The monument itself is relatively securely dated to approximately 3500 BC. If the art was applied then, one would have to think it an early example. In general, no evidence for astronomical orientation is found at the smaller surrounding monuments, the majority are instead oriented towards the central area.[6] Listoghil's context is similar to that found at Knowth and Newgrange, where a large focal passage tomb dominates smaller sites of primarily earlier date.

Overall, it would appear that Carrowmore is primarily a Type 1 passage tomb complex, the only one of this kind. Part of its importance is that it provides a snapshot of passage tomb design and construction in the period before 3500 BC. There may have been megalithic construction at the other three major passage tomb complexes in this early period also, but the dominant phase of passage tomb activity almost certainly dates to after 3500 BC in each case.

Carrowkeel

In 1911 the excavator of Carrowkeel, R. A. S. Macalister, noted the great variety in size and sophistication of its passage tombs. The diversity of monuments – from the tiny Cairn O to the sizable Cairn F – posed a problem for him: the differing scale of the monuments seemed to indicate a lengthy sequence of construction. Until relatively recently there has only been a few radiocarbon dates from Carrowkeel and those that existed have in the main indicated activity cotemporary with the construction of Newgrange and the developed phase of passage tomb construction. However, the most recent dating evidence has raised the possibility that the Carrowkeel cairns were in use several hundred years before Newgrange was constructed, perhaps as early as 3500 BC.[7] All dates from the complex are from insecure stratigraphic contexts however and, therefore, have restricted value as regards ascertaining the earliest passage tomb activity there.

The scale of and features present at the monuments are potential indicators of the sequence of construction within the complex. Carrowkeel has no clear Type 1 passage tombs, though passage tombs of small size do exist. Sites M and N are completely denuded, and unfortunately little can be said about their original form except that they had a three-recess cruciform design. Several monuments have small covering cairns (Cairns A, O and P); their status and date remain uncertain. Macalister thought the diminutive cairn A unworthy of full excavation, and found Cairn P to be chamberless. These monuments could equally be early in the internal chronology at Carrowkeel or late additions constructed subsequent to the main period of activity in the complex. However, the general impression at Carrowkeel is of mid-size Type 2 cairns; Cairns B, C, D, G and K being good examples. Among the main group of monuments, only two stones with passage tomb art have been recorded, both from Cairn B.[8] Overall, the complex seems to be primarily concerned with Type 2 activity, rituals occurring inside of the monuments away from the wider community (Fig. 8.2). Few concessions to the public are found in the architectural features at the majority of the Carrowkeel monuments, excepting perhaps Cairn F in the main group, and Heapstown in the lower ground. This latter site, approximately five kilometres from the main cluster, may be a late development (see Chapter Six). Heapstown Cairn, though unexcavated, has features that suggest it had a public-oriented focus and that it may have acted as the Type 3 monument for public ritual for the Carrowkeel complex. It is likely to have been constructed at a similar date to Newgrange and Knowth, *c.* 3200–3000 BC.

The relative absence of megalithic carving from Carrowmore and Carrowkeel is significant. It indicates a chronological dimension to passage tomb art in Ireland. Seemingly, it was not an important feature at all Type 2 sites, indicating that there may have been a slow process of development. One possibility is that the first Type 2 sites had no megalithic art, but the rituals which took place within the darkened chambers eventually prompted this creative expression. Alternatively, the lack of art at Carrowkeel could be partially explained by the unsuitability of the local stone for carving. Perhaps art was created in other materials, or painted.[9] However, in general, it appears that megalithic art was not as important at Carrowkeel as it was Loughcrew and Brú na Bóinne.

Equally, the evidence for astronomical orientation at Carrowkeel is equivocal. Most of the monuments are orientated to the north, back towards Carrowmore and the striking mass of Knocknarea Mountain on which sits Queen Maeve's tomb. Though Cairn G is visited by groups every year to witness the summer solstice sunset, it is an imprecise orientation.[10] The solar alignment may be an accidental occurrence, or perhaps an early attempt at techniques that were latterly improved upon.

Irrespective of the earliest passage tomb activity at Carrowkeel,

Figure 8.2. The Carrowkeel passage tomb complex. Cairns G and H, K and L in the foreground, Mullaghfarna and cairns O and P visible to the upper left (Con Brogan, Photographic Unit, National Monuments).

depositions were placed in the cairns in the last centuries of the fourth millennium BC (as at Carrowmore). The dynamism of the tradition may have moved to the east at this time, but the Carrowmore and Carrowkeel monuments were still active places. Nevertheless, construction and features present or absent at Carrowkeel argue that it was most associated with the second major phase of passage tomb construction.

Loughcrew

No material from any of the Loughcrew monuments have been radiocarbon dated thus far. On morphological and design grounds, however, the monuments seem to be marginally later than those at Carrowkeel. In general, the cairn diameters found at Loughcrew are greater. There is some evidence of public-oriented ritual, yet not as much as at Brú na Bóinne. A cursus-like monument is recorded nearby, though it appears to be most closely associated with the Bronze Age landscape.[11] There are several cairns of substantial diameter, most notably Cairn L and Cairn D (41 and 55 m). Nineteenth century excavations at Cairn D failed to locate a passage or chamber and hence little is known about the nature of the site or its role.

Cairn T is the focal monument for the eastern part of the complex (Fig. 8.3). Conwell recorded that, "Inside the retaining wall of large flag stones … was piled up a layer, rising from three to four feet in height, and about two feet in thickness, of broken lumps of sparkling native Irish quartz".[12] This feature which Conwell clearly indicates was inside the kerbstones and standing above them may be a precursor to the quartz wall at Newgrange (even if there is uncertainty and debate regarding the exact appearance of the wall at Newgrange and the authenticity of the reconstructed façade).[13] It also appears there were two small cairns outside the monument entrance, which may indicate stone settings similar to those found at Newgrange.[14] Without excavation it is difficult to discern whether these features were an original part of the construction, or represent a later addition. Cairn T has a probable astronomical orientation (to the equinox). Two other

Figure 8.3. Loughcrew Cairn T with Cairn S in the foreground
(photograph: Ken Williams).

sites within the complex also have astronomical arrangements: Cairn X1 which is orientated to the winter solstice sunset and Thomastown from which the sun sets behind Cairn T at the summer solstice).[15] The existence of three sites with possible astronomical arrangements at Loughcrew distinguishes it from Carrowmore and Carrowkeel and again suggests that developments there occurred at a slightly later date. Notable artefacts recovered from Loughcrew included two large polished stone balls from Cairn F and L, and basin stones from Cairns W, H, and F, and two from Cairn L.[16] Again, these late features not found at Carrowmore and Carrowkeel.

Also in contrast to Carrowmore and Carrowkeel, there is a great quantity of art at Loughcrew, indicative of a substantial artistic unfolding. The vast majority of designs are found in the inner part of the monuments. Only three kerbstones there have art, however.[17] This may indicate that internal ritual was the primary focus at least for the earlier part of the complex's history. Significantly, the styles of art found at Loughcrew do not feature the late phases of plastic art and pick-dressing in evidence at Knowth and Newgrange. It appears that the Loughcrew art is earlier in date than that at Brú na Bóinne, or at least that the complex did not experience the late flourishing which occurred in the Boyne Valley, when new art styles were adopted and earlier styles became dispensable.

Research by Shee Twohig and others has raised the prospect that several of the carved stones at Loughcrew were rock art pieces taken in from the surrounding landscape and re-used for passage tomb construction.[18] This is particularly clear at Cairn T (though also at Cairns S, V and L), where several stones have designs more usually associated with rock art, particularly cupmarks. Additionally, some of the art-covered stones are quite weathered, even though located within the chamber, indicating that they had been exposed to the elements previously. It is possible that Cairn T was a late phase Type 3 construction. It may represent an attempt to create passage tombs of greater dimensions at a time when easily available stones were already expended in previous sites, thus requiring that decorated panels be brought in from the wider landscape. Alternatively, it may have been meaningful to take these already ritually potent stones in from the wider landscape, perhaps an attempt to draw in power from those older sites.

The majority of the passage tombs at Loughcrew appear built for Type 2 ritual, as at Carrowkeel. Yet there is evidence that public-oriented ritual had a role there too, perhaps during the complex's final use period. Cairns D and L are the largest monuments in the complex and both contenders for Type 3 status (Chapter Six). Developments at Loughcrew represent a progression not apparent at Carrowmore or Carrowkeel. The elaboration of design features previously identified as the predominant feature of the second wave of passage tomb construction is best expressed there. However, the same level of monument recycling and revisionism found at Brú na Bóinne, or the latest forms of megalithic art, are not in evidence. One wonders whether signature features associated with late phase activity at Brú na Bóinne were in some instances added to the Loughcrew monuments as *post hoc* additions, most notably perhaps the stone settings, quartz wall and kerbstone art at Cairn T? Or was the complex itself reconstituted for public ritual?

The huge Cairn D could be significant in this regard. It is by far the largest cairn in the complex. At 55 m in diameter, it approaches the scale of the larger Brú na Bóinne monuments. Notably, a large quartz pillar stood to its north-west.[19] Yet after three weeks of excavation, with a team of between twelve and twenty men at various points, Conwell could not find an internal structure.[20] Was it intended to superficially mimic the super-sites of Brú na Bóinne, perhaps an attempt to emulate them through scale alone? We do not know whether the late phase passage tombs in the north-west, Queen Maeve's tomb or Heapstown Cairn, contain passage tombs but it cannot be ruled out that, like Cairn D at Loughcrew, they are without internal features and mirror Newgrange only outwardly.

Brú na Bóinne

The Boyne complex seems completely dominated by late phase monuments and features. Our impressions may be somewhat skewed by the more epic structures, however; this complex probably had a much longer history. Indeed, the Early Neolithic house activity uncovered during excavations at Knowth might suggest that the Brú na Bóinne complex had a longer use-period than any of the other complexes. If passage tombs were also constructed at the same time, or soon after those early houses, it is not inconceivable that there was eight hundred years of megalithic construction at Brú na Bóinne.

Nevertheless, the incredible level of activity there between 3200 and 2900 BC means that earlier activity stands a high chance of having been removed; earlier sites cannibalised for the construction of new passage tombs. Passage tombs from earlier periods are highly unlikely to have survived given the quantity and scale of the developed monuments. The possibility of Type 1 passage tombs nearby on the Dublin coast, and those sites already discussed on the west coast of Britain may even support the possibility of early phase passage tombs in the Boyne region, though ultimately this must remain an open question. More certain is the existence of Type 2 monuments. Though many of the passage tombs surrounding the focal monuments are undated, sufficient evidence exists to indicate that some are earlier than Newgrange.[21] At Knowth, Sites 16 and 13 were demonstrably earlier. The builders had to adjust the curve of the main mound to accommodate Site 13 and the new construction also required that the entrance to Site 16 be remodelled to maintain access.[22] Additionally, Site L at Newgrange revealed evidence of earlier activity underneath its cairn.[23] This significant site, and others nearby, would probably be given greater consideration if they were not in the shadow of one of the largest passage tombs in western Europe. Newgrange and Knowth, as noted previously, are also likely to have been constructed from at least one earlier monument (Type 2 sites?), again demonstrating earlier phases within the complex. It is probable that a passage tomb centre of some importance existed at Brú na Bóinne, before the largest monuments were built.

Newgrange and Knowth are the most investigated sites at Brú na Bóinne and have the greatest number of radiocarbon dates.[24] Even without those dates it would be clear from their morphology, scale and sophistication that they are late in the tradition. Developments associated with public ritual also have their greatest currency at Brú na Bóinne. Even some of the smaller tombs have features that are associated with later ritual, notably the basin stone at Knowth Site 2 and the stone setting in front of Site 4.[25] Eight of the small satellites around Knowth had at least one decorated kerbstone. Stout uses the term 'inclusive' features to describe these aspects of construction.[26] Again, it is not clear whether these basins and stone settings were early instances of the use of these novel ritual features, perhaps created before Knowth and Newgrange, or features that were added-on as they became more important during the construction of later monuments. It would seem the hallmarks of the developed phase of passage tomb construction are stamped all over the Boyne Valley complex. Accepting there has not been as much excavation at the other complexes, it is still notable that these features are not found to the same extent elsewhere.

As noted previously, Brú na Bóinne is somewhat removed in its landscape setting, cordoned off by rivers on all sides. This 'inland-island' though perhaps not as physically isolated as Carrowkeel or Loughcrew complexes, still maintained a separation from the wider community. Nevertheless, it is on low ground (only 60 m above sea level at its highest point) and relatively accessible. Hence, its isolation was in all possibility more symbolic than physical, and cultural prohibitions may have served to emphasise the separateness of this complex. If it had an earlier history as a Type 2 complex, a time must have come where prohibitions were lifted as Brú na Bóinne began a transformation into a public-oriented ritual centre. Restrictions or prohibitions which once existed may have eased as the complex moved into the later phases of passage tomb construction and ceremony, as so many people would have had to be present around the site for the movement of materials and construction.

The end of passage tomb construction was, in turn, followed by various developments between 2900 and 2500 BC, which fall outside the scope of this book.[27] Brú na Bóinne remained an incredibly active place. Newgrange, Knowth and Dowth were still important foci of attention, but new passage tombs were no longer constructed. After 2900 BC the monuments, rituals, and art of the previous centuries had fallen out of favour. Grooved ware, a pottery type closely associated with the Orkney Islands, became prevalent. Large embanked enclosures, pit circles and timber circles came to dominate at Newgrange, and in the wider landscape. The entrance to Newgrange may have been sealed in this period. New rituals took place in monuments open to the sky. No more would light be looked for or found in the dark.

Brú na Bóinne had a long history. Though much of that activity may be masked by the intense activity in the period Newgrange and Knowth were constructed, it still perhaps had the longest history of the main four complexes. It contained and still contains many monuments of moderate scale, and probably had an important phase where Type 2 ritual was prevalent, but its signature phase was a period of intense development from 3200–2900 BC, when new developments in construction and styles of art occurred, novelties which were not replicated to the same degree or intensity at any of the other major Irish passage tomb complexes.

Removing the scaffold

There is much about passage tombs we do not know, even regarding basic construction procedures. For example, megalithic sites probably had temporary elements for which no evidence remains. Some probably required wooden scaffolding or other supportive structures during their construction. O'Kelly put considerable thought into trying to reconstruct the building methods and sequence of construction at Newgrange and concluded that scaffolding, vertical timbers, planks, levers, rollers and wedges were all employed.[28] The builders would have dismantled or disposed of these elements when the megalithic elements were completed. The model of three types of passage tombs presented in this book is similar in some respects. It is a tool whose primary role is to help in the identification of broad changes over time, patterns of growth and development within the tradition; the monuments to be seen afresh. However, developments in this tradition of megalithic construction were manifold and will never be adequately captured by these, inevitably crude categorisations. Indeed, each of the three types of passage tomb presented here, in particular Type 2, represent a large group of monuments within which sub-groups could be identified – if one's ambition was purely that of categorisation. Moreover, several Irish passage tombs within and outside of the main complexes do not fit neatly into this categorisation.

Sites such as the Mound of the Hostages and Fourknocks I and II, Co. Meath, Millin Bay, Co. Donegal, and Cairn E at Carrowkeel, have features particular to those monuments.[29] The Mound of the Hostages, for instance, has no kerbstones at the base of its cairn, but a most peculiar surrounding feature: seventeen pits containing small deposits of cremated bone. Fourknocks I may originally have been an open-air site before it was transformed into a chambered tomb. Notably, its chamber area is significantly bigger than all other Irish passage tombs, its floor space more than twice as large as at Newgrange (42 m^2). Fourknocks II may also have begun life as an open-air monument but, unusually, is focused on what may have been a cremation trench. Millin Bay was constructed over a stone wall. First a long cist was built to one side of the wall which was subsequently covered in an oval mound, the wall extending out from this at either end. This site also has forms of megalithic art that differ somewhat from the most familiar styles in the passage tomb tradition. Cairn E at Carrowkeel has a long cairn (40×11 m), a feature more typically associated with court tombs, yet attached to a relatively standard passage tomb chamber. As should be apparent from these brief descriptions, each passage tomb had its own individual history worthy of investigation and study. While Newgrange can be seen as representative of a stage of passage tomb development and compared with somewhat similar sites, there is no doubt it is also unique – no precise equivalent exists.

In what follows, like a wooden scaffold that has served its role, the three types of passage tomb model will be left to one side and the origins, meanings and role of Newgrange discussed from a more fluid perspective.

An Archaeology of the Otherworld

Newgrange was conceived and erected towards the end of a long tradition of monuments dedicated to the religious needs of Neolithic communities; an archaeological odyssey, from small-scale sites built by early farming groups, to potent otherworld centres where ritual training took place at the edge of society, eventually to temple-like monuments standing at the heart of the religious and political sphere in Neolithic Ireland. It is but the tip of a great iceberg.

Can we say why Newgrange was built? Professor O'Kelly once stated that, "As a generalisation you can't think of Newgrange without thinking of Religion".[1] It is difficult to argue with this statement. Yet religion is a problematic term as it difficult to define or separate as a discrete element of culture.[2] Perhaps a less contentious way to consider religion is through what it does rather than what it is. Robert Bellah has proposed that one of religion's most important aspects is that it allows people to create other realities, other worlds.[3] Imagination and creative thinking are defining qualities of humanity, which separate us from other species. It is largely because of humanity's creative convictions that great monuments like Stonehenge, the Pyramids of Giza exist or Newgrange and the passage tombs of Ireland exist.

Maurice Bloch refers to the results of this imaginative capacity as the *transcendental social* as opposed to the *transactional* social of everyday survival, meaning that certain concepts and ideas can transcend the society that gives birth to them.[4] An example might be kingship, or democracy, ideas which can stand above individuals and times: the queen is dead, long live the queen. The idea of an otherworld, imminent and approachable, is a transcendental concept that I think applied to all phases of passage tomb construction.

How was this otherworld conceived? Who or what resided there? How did it impact on this world? Confusion sometimes arises as to whether passage tombs were straightforward burial places, or instead, were more concerned with ancestral beings; and again, whether those sometimes nebulously framed ancestors were genealogical ones or mythical ones, gods or spirits. Bloch suggests that all these beings belong to what he calls a *transcendental network*.[5] As gods, spirits, mythical and genealogical ancestors are all equally mysterious and invisible, effectively, they are also equally transcendent. Newgrange was a pivotal part of a powerful transcendental network; of a chain of monuments which had acted as bridges to other worlds. They facilitated engagement with ancestral presences and perhaps to other invisible beings over hundreds of years of passage tomb construction. Paradoxically, it appears this seeming obsession with the otherworld began to take on an increasingly public/this-world focus over time.

The most westerly complex, Carrowmore, appears to have been in use half a millennium before Newgrange was built. During the early stages of passage tomb construction, the greatest concern of those communities seems to have been the deposition of select human remains into the monuments. This may have taken place on a seasonal or yearly basis, perhaps in association with the death of individuals from a particular lineage. A connection with the sea was paramount. This may hint at the location of settlements, but may also point to beliefs of these communities. The otherworld may have been thought to reside over the sea. Perhaps memories or tales about the homeland of early immigrants melded with religious conceptions in envisioning their spiritual homeland as seaward, or the sea as a passage to other realms.

We know very little else about what kind of religious beliefs these groups may have had. They may have had spiritual beliefs around quartz and rock crystal, as this material is often found in the monuments chambers.[6] Some form of shamanism may have occurred in the society that built these small tombs, but if so, this was most likely closer to 'vertical shamanism' than 'horizontal shamanism': that is, shamanistic practitioners probably did not have an esteemed position above other members of society, or were not especially connected with secular authority in a complex ranked society.[7]

As the climate deteriorated, newer and more beneficent structures were built to honour the ancestors. Close relations with the sun and its cycles were established by constructing monuments with solar orientations. Individuals may have been selected to go through the challenges associated with becoming ritual specialists. Perhaps these people were distinguished in some way through heredity, individual talents, illness or an unusual physical feature that could mark them out in some way. People that entered passage tombs may have been seen to be acquiring knowledge in the otherworld that ultimately would guide their communities. It was they who consulted with the gods; it was they who knew the course of the sun; it was they who went down into the underworld, the place of water and seeds. This necessitated the construction of more monuments that would facilitate these experiences. The evidence suggests that some kind of perception-altering rite was taking place in passage tombs of this form. Art found inside the chambers were meant only for the select group within. Altered states may have been induced by long periods of seclusion in darkness. Cycles of the sun, seasonal celebration, cycles of life, and perhaps ideas around reincarnation, may have been some the areas around which this growing religion was founded. Imagistic rites would have fused the parties involved with strong ties. Those that interceded with the otherworld powers became conduits of sacred authority; they spoke for the deities (or whatever aspects of the transcendental network they communed with inside passage tomb chambers).

Finally, great public monuments like Newgrange were built at the most important locations within these religious centres. These developed passage tombs have features associated with previous monuments – *e.g.*, cairns, passages, chambers, recesses, art, astronomical alignments – but they were used differently. The outside of the cairn was re-imagined with public ceremony in mind. Art intended for public consumption embellished the exterior of the structure.

Older passage tombs could be demolished for materials to build public-oriented structures, monuments constructed on a scale never seen before. Other materials were retrieved from afar, work which would have brought distant peoples together. The sizeable groups necessary for construction purposes, and the crowds present for ceremony at Newgrange, may have had a dysphoric effect, engendering unity of purpose between otherwise anonymous groups. Ritual and ceremony seem to be approaching that of doctrinal religiosity: repeat ritual involving large groups. A sacerdotal class was almost certainly present. Specialist artisans were charged with creating art. Large anonymous groups participated in the construction of these sites and made seasonal pilgrimages for ceremonial purposes. The rhythm of the year, including the journey of the sun, seems to have been the bedrock of ceremony. Ritual training may still have taken place at the more modest structures within the complexes, but the ritual focus had changed and large public gatherings came to dominate. In this way these passage tomb centres facilitated societal transformation.

The sacerdotal role may have become more and more politicised as questions of power and leadership may have been resolved alongside older passage tomb ritual. The people who interceded with the otherworld powers may have held powerful positions in society. Recesses, which in lesser passage tombs could have been used for people to occupy for religious training, were now taken up with large basins; their previous role amended for this new context. The burials which occurred may have been those of people of political power, perhaps the families of ruling lineages. More accomplished, prestigious, objects were placed on their pyres. The construction of great monuments, the burial and validation of leaders and leadership claims, and celebration of great turning points in nature including the rebirth of the sun at the winter solstice may all have been intimately associated. There may have been some form of procession between Newgrange, Knowth and Dowth. The cursus terminal at Newgrange and linear route way leading north-west from Dowth by the Ballinacrad linear monument may be relevant here.

Eventually passage tombs go out of use. We do not know why this happened. It may be that an upturn in the weather, combined with new influences from northern Britain, ushered in changes in society. The role of the passage tombs was minimised, their entrances eventually covered over. If concerns about deteriorating climate had been one of the factors in the evolution of passage tomb construction, then the necessity for the construction of new monuments may have decreased as more favourable conditions prevailed. Perhaps older passage tomb ritual had run its course, or was thought to have fulfilled its purpose as more favourable conditions returned. Some writers have written of the intentional slighting of Newgrange, whereby the entrance to the passage may have been purposely sealed by additions of cairn material.[8] Perhaps there were suspicions around activities which took place in the dark, away from the public gaze, or of figures who may have harnessed ancient ritual for their own advancement. Yet Newgrange continued to resonate, as can be observed through the considerable activity around it down through time. Indeed, passage tombs like Newgrange still resonate for many people today.

As noted at the beginning of this book, Newgrange has become emblematic of Ireland. The reconstruction of Newgrange was in part a reconstruction of Irish identity. Like the shaman who travelled to other realms to bring back lost souls, M. J. O'Kelly travelled into prehistory to retrieve a particularly bright part of the Irish narrative, which had long been lost. The light which shines into Newgrange every winter solstice is a symbol of the tremendous skill and creativity of our Irish and European ancestors, and creates a bridge between those people and us. The winter solstice light at Newgrange allows us to see a little of their world; we see something they saw, if through modern eyes. What was Newgrange for? The builders told us: it was about light; it was about the sun; it was about life. The wonder is that their message was delivered. This could only happen because of the knowledge and skills gained through hundreds of years of imagining and constructing similar monuments. It is that tremendous ability, and the powerful vision that lay behind it, which has allowed Newgrange and similar sites to survive and permit us to see something of their story. Newgrange was not the first light, or the only light, but it undoubtedly was one of the brightest.

Notes

Introduction

1. O'Kelly 1982, 7.
2. *Ibid.*, 100–1 and plate 52.
3. For Knowth see Eogan 1998; Eogan forthcoming. For Dowth see Eogan 2009.
4. *E.g.* Herity 1974; Herity and Eogan 1977.
5. Lynch 1969; 1975; 2000; Sheridan 1986.
6. O'Sullivan 1993a, 8.
7. Scarre 2011, 138.
8. L'Helgouach 1965.
9. Though see Piggott 1954, 220–222.
10. Iberia arguably has the best comparative material, see Piggott 154, 221; Eogan 1979; 1986, 170–2.
11. Shee Twohig 1981.
12. For passage tomb chronology in Brittany see Scarre 2011, 76 and 145. For Irish dates see Smyth 2009; Cooney *et al.* 2011; Bayliss and O'Sullivan 2013; Bergh and Hensey 2013a and b. Please note that all radiocarbon dates in this text should be considered calibrated unless otherwise stated. Details of the methods, laboratories and so on can be found in the cited publications.

Chapter 1

1. Recent investigations at both Newgrange and Dowth have discovered traces of additional passage tombs in those vicinities (Joe Fenwick, Conor Brady and Steve Davis pers. comm.).
2. McCann 1993; 1994. An upper limit of thirty-two Loughcrew passage tombs is possible, Lynda McCormack (pers. comm.).
3. Hensey *et al.* 2014, Table A.1.
4. Bergh 1995; Hensey and Bergh 2013.

5. Curran-Mulligan 1994; Hensey and Robin 2011.
6. Ó Nualláin 1968.
7. Rynne 1960.
8. This figure is an estimate comprised of 236 positively identified passage tombs (Shee Twohig 2004, 8), plus unopened cairns that contextually are likely to be passage tombs. Sheridan (1986) for instance makes reference to twenty such cairns.
9. Conwell 1866, 378.
10. Petrie 1838. Wood-Martin 1888.
11. Macalister *et al.* 1912.
12. Wood-Martin 1888, 9.
13. Herity 1974; Herity and Eogan 1977; Eogan 1986, fig. 89.
14. Renfrew 1973.
15. Burenhult 1980, 14.
16. Burenhult 1980; 1984; 2003; 2005.
17. See Caulfield 1983; Woodman 2000; Sheridan 2003c for arguments against the Mesolithic construction interpretation.
18. Bergh and Hensey 2013a and b.
19. Bayliss in Bergh and Hensey 2013a.
20. Ghilardi and O'Connell 2013a, b, c; O'Connell *et al.* 2014.
21. Cooney *et al.* 2011; Whitehouse, N. J. *et al.* 2014.
22. Bergh 1995, 67.
23. Bergh 1995, 79–81.
24. Burenhult 1980; 2009.
25. *E.g.*, Cooney *et al.* 2011; Whitehouse N. J. *et al.* 2014; McClatchie *et al.* 2014.
26. Stolze 2012a and b; Stolze *et al.* 2013a; Stolze *et al.* 2013b; Ghilardi and O'Connell 2013a, b, c; Whitehouse, N. J. *et al.* 2014; McClatchie *et al.* 2014; O'Connell *et al.* 2014.
27. Smyth 2014; McSparron 2008.
28. Whitehouse, N. J. *et al.* 2014; McClatchie *et al.* 2014. For manuring see Bogaard *et al.* 2007; Fraser *et al.* 2011.
29. Bergh 1995, 122.
30. Aldridge 1965, 14.
31. Herity 1974, fig. 56 and 279.
32. Cody 1987; 1988.
33. Sheridan 2003b.
34. Herity 1974, 72.
35. McGuinness 1995.

36. Shee Twohig 1995.
37. Lynch 1969; 1975; 2000; Sheridan 2000; 2003a and b. These monuments were once referred to as B-Dolmens, *e.g.*, Daniel 1950, 95; Herity 1974.
38. Lynch 1975, 31.
39. Richie 1970.
40. Sheridan 2000.
41. Sheridan *et al.* 2008; Schulting in Lynch 2014.
42. Radford 1958.
43. Smith and Lynch 1987; Lynch 2000, 73; Sheridan 2003a and b.
44. Sheridan 2010, 95.
45. Whitehouse, N. J. *et al.* 2014.
46. Herity 1974, 279.
47. Based on an estimate of two hundred and sixty passage tombs, see Note 8 above.
48. Barrett 1988; Bradley 1998, 62.
49. *E.g.* Jones 2007; Tilley 2008, ch. 5.
50. Hensey 2010, 269–70.
51. This is evident in the Maltese Neolithic, for example, where sites may have been aligned to the north-west so as to harken back across the sea to islands from where Malta was first settled and prized lithic resources originated (Stoddart *et al.* 1993; *cf.* Robb 2001).

Chapter 2

1. Dark and Gent 2001; Whitehouse, N. J. *et al.* 2014.
2. *E.g.*, Sheridan 1986.
3. See Bergh 1995; Hensey and Bergh 2013.
4. Mitchell 1984, 1995.
5. Fieldwalking has indicated high densities of lithics in the landscape near Newgrange (especially to its south and east), potentially reflecting considerable settlement activity, but also that a 'zone of exclusion' may have existed around the monument itself, see Brady 2007, 216.
6. Bayliss and O'Sullivan 2013, 98.
7. Ongoing project involving the author, T. Kador, J. Geber, P. Meehan and S. Moore.
8. Cooney *et al.* 2011; Bayliss and O'Sullivan 2013.
9. At least three passage tombs in the Carrowkeel complex (Cairns B, G and H) display evidence of revetments within their mounds.
10. See Hensey 2014.

11. Coffey 1898.
12. Ruggles and Saunders 1993, 3.
13. *E.g.*, Jones and MacGregor 2002; Tilley 2004; Scarre and Lawson 2006.
14. Jones 1999, 344.
15. Card and Thomas 2012; Ramírez *et al.* 2015.
16. Lynch 1998.
17. O'Sullivan 2004, 48.
18. Turner 1967.
19. Tilley 1996.
20. Jones 1999.
21. Watson and Keating 2000.
22. Watson 2001, 180.
23. Devereux and Jahn 1996; *cf.* Watson and Keating 2000, 262.
24. Macalister 1932; Herity 1974; Eogan 1986; Bergh 1995.
25. Danaher 1972; Ó hÓgáin 1999.
26. Cook 1914.
27. Patrick 1974; Ray 1989.
28. Dehn and Hansen 2006.
29. Prendergast 2011a.
30. Shee 1973.
31. O'Sullivan 2006.
32. Robin 2009.
33. Hensey and Robin 2011; 2012.
34. C. O'Kelly 1973; Shee Twohig 1981, 112.
35. Eogan 1986, 167–8.
36. O'Sullivan 2006.
37. See Hensey 2012.
38. Vallancey 1786, 211–12.
39. Jones 2004, 202.
40. Shee Twohig 2000.
41. Eogan 1997; 1999.
42. O'Sullivan 1986; 1989; 1993a; 1997; 2006.

Chapter 3

1. Eliade 1956, 177.
2. Mooney 1896, 716.
3. Whittle 1996, 1.
4. Davies and Robb 2004.

5. Mills and Slobodin 1994.
6. Hensey 2014.
7. Robin 2010, 414.
8. Ereira 2009.
9. Schwimmer 1973; Iteanu 1990, 47.
10. Bradley 1989; Patton 1990; Lewis-Williams and Dowson 1993; Dronfield 1995a; 1995b; 1996a; 1996b.
11. Dronfield 1995a; 1995b; Lewis-Williams and Pearce 2005.
12. O'Sullivan 1996b, 59.
13. Kerri Cleary, pers. comm.
14. Lewis-Williams and Pearce 2005; Dronfield 1996b.
15. Kehoe 2000.
16. Humphrey 1995.
17. Francfort and Hamayon 2003.
18. Whitehouse 1996; 2000; 2004; Whitehouse and Martin 2004.
19. Whitehouse *et al.* 2014, 136.
20. Whitehouse and Hodder 2010; Whitehouse *et al.* 2014.
21. Whitehouse 2000.
22. Whitehouse 2004, 63.
23. Whitehouse 2004, 106–11.
24. Whitehouse 1996.
25. Whitehouse 2004, 63.
26. Swann *et al.* 2012.
27. Whitehouse 2004.

Chapter 4

1. O'Kelly's 1982, 123.
2. Prendergast 2011a.
3. Prendergast 2011a.
4. Prendergast 2009; 2011b.
5. O'Sullivan 2004.
6. Prendergast 2011a.
7. Burrow 2010.
8. Patton *et al.* 1999.
9. Frank Prendergast, pers. comm.
10. Hensey 2008.
11. Hemp 1930, 188; Burrows 2010, 261.
12. Mackie 1997, 344; Challands *et al.* 2005.

13. United Nations Report 2007.
14. Renfrew 1984, 178–80; Richards 1996; Ruggles 1999, 154.
15. Moroney 1999, 14.
16. Ingold 2000, 253.
17. Eliasson 2003.
18. Eliasson 1997.
19. May 2003.

Chapter 5

1. As an example, there is a widespread recognition that evidence of ritual feasting can be found in the archaeological record but fasting, which has an equally important role in religious practices (especially in rites de passage), leaves no trace. See Dietler 2011, 187.
2. Tilley 2008, 130–2.
3. Mitchell 1984; 1995.
4. Stout 2002, 113–15.
5. *E.g.* Schulting and Richards 2002; Richards *et al.* 2003; Schulting 2013; Schulting *et al.* in Lynch forthcoming.
6. John Waddell, pers. comm.
7. Lynch forthcoming.
8. Lynch forthcoming. A crab apple endocarp returned a radiocarbon date of 3340–3029 cal BC (UB-23059: 4478±32).
9. Robert Bergin, pers. comm.
10. Clare Tuffy, pers. comm.
11. Greenhalgh 2005, 77.
12. William Roche pers. comm.
13. Roberts 2007.
14. Quinn *et al.* 2006.
15. Boas 1909; Goldman 1975; Roche and McHutchison 1998 .
16. Mitchell 1992; Meighan *et al.* 2002; Meighan *et al.* 2003; George Sevastopulo, pers. comm.
17. Stout and Stout 2008, 8.
18. Philips *et al.* 2001; 2002.
19. George Sevastopulo, pers. comm.
20. Stout and Stout 2008, 8 and Fig. 7.
21. Conor Brady, pers. comm.
22. Brady 2007, 216.
23. O'Kelly 1982, 215. Additionally a cowrie shell was recovered from the

northern quadrant of the central chamber, NMI number E56.951, see O'Kelly 1982, 196.

24. McCormick 1986, 39.
25. Newenham 1839 cited in Herity 1974, 173.
26. McCormick 1986.
27. Herity 1974, 172.
28. Raftery 2009; O'Neill 2013.
29. Burenhult 1980, 32.
30. Macalister *et al.* 1912; see Hensey *et al.* 2014 for discussion.
31. Thomas 2003; Fowler and Cummings 2003.
32. Hemp 1930; 1936; Lynch 1969.
33. Powell and Daniel 1956.
34. Wood-Martin 1888, Fig. 31.
35. Burenhult 1980; 2009.
36. Jones and Richards 2003.
37. Cassen 2000; 2005; 2009; Whittle 2000.
38. Dave Wall, pers. comm.
39. Wilson and Berrow 2006, 41.
40. Dave Wall of the Irish Whale and Dolphin Group has noted (pers. comm.) that: "of the whale species which occur or occurred in Irish waters, it most resembles a humpback whale due to what appears like a long pectoral fin". Dave is one Ireland's most experienced offshore cetacean surveyors.
41. http://www.iwdg.ie/index.php?option=com_k2andview=itemandid =2027 (accessed o1/02/15).
42. Hensey 2012.
43. Robin 2012.
44. Harbison 2003, 111. It seems several archaeologists have considered this art as representational. Herity (1974, fig. 107) for instance, saw it as a *marmite* or axe symbol; notably Stout 2002, 53 referred to it as 'dolphin-like'.

Chapter 6

1. Cooney 2000, 19.
2. C. O'Kelly 1978, 104.
3. O'Kelly 1979; 1982, 72–3; Simpson 1988, 35; Cooney 2006, 705; Eriksen 2006; 2008; Stout and Stout 2008; Eogan 2010, 28; Lynch forthcoming.
4. This is so not only in the north-west but at the Antrim sites too. See Conclusion Note 6.

5. Bergh 1995, 246, Appendix illustration 35; Rotherham 1895, 311.
6. C. O'Kelly 1982, 146.
7. Eogan 1999, 417; 2006, 138 ; Thomas 1990; 1992; Jones 2007; Tilley 2008.
8. Eogan 1986, 178.
9. Hensey and Robin 2011. The kerbstones with art at Loughcrew are Cairn T, K29, Cairn H, K8 and Cairn X1, K1.
10. Newman 1999.
11. Condit 1997.
12. Cooney 2000, 158.
13. Corlett 2014.
14. Herity 1974, 136.
15. Eogan 1982, 141.
16. Shee Twohig *et al.* 2010. It can be difficult to adjudicate between a basin and a paving or flagstone, both features occupy a similar position in the recess.
17. Eogan 1986, 116.
18. Sheridan 1986, 25.
19. Wilde 1857, 186.
20. O'Sullivan 1993b; 1995; 1996a; 2004.
21. O'Sullivan 2004.
22. O'Sullivan 2005; Bayliss and O'Sullivan 2013; Schulting *et al.* in Lynch forthcoming.
23. Whittle 1996, 247–8.
24. O'Sullivan 2005.
25. Conwell 1873, 49–50.
26. Walshe 1941.
27. Whitehouse, N. J. *et al.* 2014.
28. Walshe 1941; Childe 1940, 65; Piggott 1954, 199; Shee Twohig 1981, 223.
29. Hensey and Robin 2011.
30. Harbison 1988, 57.
31. Bergh 2002.
32. Bergh 1995, fig. 5:16; 238–9.
33. O'Kelly 1982, 122.
34. McClatchie *et al.* 2014.
35. Stolze 2013b.
36. Ghilardi and O'Connell 2012; 2013a, b and c; Stolze 2012 a and b; Stolze *et al.* 2012; Stolze *et al.* 2013a; Stolze *et al.* 2013b.
37. Stolze 2013b, 157.
38. Sheridan 1986; *cf.* Lewis-Williams and Pearce 2005.

39. Brady 2007.
40. Fraser 1998.
41. Scarre 1998, 182.
42. Brück 2005, 61.
43. Barnard and Woodburn 1988, 24.
44. Eogan 1986, 218.
45. Whitehouse 2004, ch. 5.
46. Whitehouse 2000.
47. Whitehouse and Hodder 2010; also see Whitehouse and Martin 2004.
48. Whitehouse, N. *et al.* 2014, 134.
49. Cooney 2000, 88.
50. Whitehouse 2004, 9.
51. Whitehouse 2004, ch. 5.
52. Whitehouse, N. *et al.* 2014, 134.
53. Whitehouse 2004, Table 4.1.
54. Eogan 1992; Bradley 2007; Carlin forthcoming.
55. Eogan 1979; 1986; 1990; 1999; O'Sullivan 1997; 2006.

Chapter 7

1. Hensey 2012.
2. Eogan 1986, 148; C. O'Kelly 1978, 128; 1982 147–8; Stout and Stout 2008, 22.
3. Robin 2009.
4. Shee Twohig 2000; Stout and Stout 2008; Lynch forthcoming.
5. O'Kelly 1982, 182–5; Shee Twohig 2000, 97.
6. Shee Twohig 2000.
7. C. O'Kelly 1982, 180, fig. 50.
8. C. O'Kelly 1978, 126.
9. Powell and Daniel 1956, 47; O'Kelly 1964.
10. Ó Ríordáin and Daniel 1964, 77; Herity 1974, 186; C. O'Kelly 1978; O'Kelly *et al.* 1978, 325.
11. Wilde 1849, 199–200.
12. Powell 1994, 95; Eogan 1998; Thomas 1990, 174–5; Shee Twohig 2000.
13. O'Sullivan 1993a, 17.
14. C. O'Kelly 1982, 150.
15. C. O'Kelly 1978, 130.
16. Cochrane 2009.
17. C. O'Kelly 1978, 129–31.

18. Shee 1973, 164.
19. O'Kelly and O'Kelly 1983.
20. *E.g.* O'Sullivan 2006.
21. C. O'Kelly 1982, 130.
22. Whitehouse 2004, 73.
23. C. O'Kelly 1982, 147–8.
24. C. O'Kelly 1978, 126.
25. Eogan 1986, 186.
26. O'Kelly 1982, 92.
27. Lynch forthcoming
28. Lynch forthcoming.
29. Schulting in Lynch forthcoming.
30. Eriksen 2008.
31. Lynch forthcoming; O'Kelly 1973, 138; 1982, 85–92 proposed that turves may have been intentional positioned as a way to stabilise the cairn and relieve pressure on particular structural features.
32. Fergusson 1872, 205–6.
33. Lynch forthcoming.
34. O'Kelly 1982, plate 38.
35. The cow tooth was dated to 2564–2298 cal BC (UB-25186), see Lynch forthcoming.
36. Lynch forthcoming.
37. Eogan 2010, 8 has also concluded that there are three primary phases at Newgrange.

Chapter 8

1. Bergh and Hensey 2013a; Hensey *et al.* 2014.
2. Cooney 2000, 158.
3. Bergh 1995; Fraser 1998; Cooney 2000, 152–74; Eogan forthcoming.
4. Fraser 1998.
5. Hensey and Robin 2011.
6. See Meehan 2012 for discussion of a potential seasonal orientation at Listoghil.
7. For dating evidence from Carrowkeel up to 2014 and dates contemporary with the developed phase in the Boyne Valley see Hensey *et al.* 2014 and Kador *et al.* forthcoming. The new dating programme forms part of an ongoing project by the author, T. Kador, J. Geber, P. Meehan and S. Moore.

8. Hensey and Robin 2011; 2012.
9. Piggott 1954, 222; Ó Ríordáin and Daniel, 1964, 54; Eogan 1986, 148; Card and Thomas 2012; Ramírez *et al.* 2015.
10. See Hensey 2008.
11. Newman 1995; 1999.
12. Conwell 1873, 30.
13. Eriksen 2006; 2008; Cooney 2006; Stout and Stout 2008; Lynch forthcoming.
14. Rotherham 1895, 311.
15. Prendergast 2009; Prendergast 2011b.
16. Conwell 1866; 1873.
17. The three examples are: Cairn T, K29; Cairn H, K8; Cairn X1, K1.
18. Shee Twohig *et al.* 2010.
19. Conwell 1873, 50.
20. Conwell 1873, 49–50.
21. Eogan 1984; 1986; Cooney, 2000, 158; Schulting *et al.* in Eogan forthcoming.
22. Eogan 1984, 79 and 109; Eogan 1986, plate 27; Eogan 1998, 170.
23. O'Kelly *et al.* 1978.
24. For a summary see Smyth (ed.) 2009; Eogan forthcoming.
25. Eogan 1984.
26. Stout 2010.
27. See Cooney 2000; Carlin forthcoming.
28. O'Kelly 1982, 120. Also see Eogan 1986, 217.
29. Macalister *et al.* 1912; Collins and Waterman 1955; Hartnett 1957; 1971; O'Sullivan 2005.

Conclusion

1. Roy 1986, 40.
2. Bradley 2005.
3. Bellah 2011.
4. Bloch 2008.
5. Bloch 2008.
6. In the course of fieldwork the author has found quartz in Type 1 passage tomb chambers in north Antrim. This suggests a degree of additional significance for this stone as large quantities of high quality flint was abundant in this locality.
7. Hugh-Jones 1996.
8. Eriksen 2006; 2008; Simpson 1988, 35.

References

Aldridge, R. B. 1965. Megalithic and other sites in counties Mayo and Galway. *Journal of the Galway Archaeological and Historical Society 1964–65* 31, 11–15.

Barrett, J. C. 1988. The living, the dead and the ancestors: Neolithic and Early Bronze Age mortuary practices. In J. Barrett and I. Kinnes (eds) *The archaeology of context in the Neolithic and Bronze Age: Recent Trends*, 30–41. Sheffield: Department of Archaeology and Prehistory.

Bayliss, A. and O'Sullivan, M. 2013. Interpreting chronologies for the Mound of the Hostages, Tara and its contemporary contexts in Neolithic and Bronze Age Ireland. In M. O'Sullivan, C. Scarre and M. Doyle (eds) *Tara – from the Past to the Future*, 26–104. Dublin: Wordwell.

Bellah, R. 2011. *Religion in Human Evolution: From the Paleolithic to the Axial Age*. Cambridge MA: Harvard University Press.

Bergh, S. 1995. *Landscape of the Monuments. A study of the passage tombs in the Cúil Irra region, Co. Sligo, Ireland*. Stockholm: Riksantikvarieämbetet Arkeologiska Undersökningar.

Bergh, S. 2002. Knocknarea – the ultimate monument: megaliths and mountains in Neolithic Cúil Irra, north-west Ireland. In C. Scarre (ed.) *Monuments and Landscape in Atlantic Europe*, 107–21. London: Routledge.

Bergh, S. and Hensey, R. 2013a. Unpicking the chronology of Carrowmore. *Oxford Journal of Archaeology* 32(4), 343–66.

Bergh, S. and Hensey, R. 2013b. The Neolithic Dates from Carrowmore 1978–98: A source critical review. doi: http://aran.library.nuigalway.ie/xmlui/handle/10379/3570

Barnard, A. and Woodburn, J. 1988. Introduction. In T. Ingold, D. Riches and J. Woodburn (eds) *Hunters and Gatherers 2. Property, power and ideology*, 4–32. Oxford: Berg.

Bloch, M. 2008. Why religion is nothing special but is central. *Philosophical Transactions of the Royal Society B: Biological Sciences*, 363(1499), 2055–61.

Boas, F. 1909. The Kwakiutl of Vancouver Island. *Bulletin of the American Museum of Natural History* 8, 301–522.

Bogaard, A., Heaton, T. H. E., Poulton, P. and Merbach, I. 2007. The impact of manuring on nitrogen isotope ratios in cereals: archaeological implications for reconstruction of diet and crop management practices. *Journal of Archaeological Science* 34, 335–43.

Bradley, R. 1989. Darkness and light in the design of megalithic tombs. *Oxford Journal of Archaeology* 8(3), 251–59.

Bradley, R. 1998. *The Significance of Monuments.* London: Routledge.

Bradley, R. 2005. *Ritual and Domestic Life in Prehistoric Europe.* Abington: Routledge.

Bradley, R. 2007. *The Prehistory of Britain and Ireland.* Cambridge: Cambridge University Press.

Brady, C. 2007. The lithic landscape of the Newgrange environs: an introduction. In M. Larsson and M. Parker Pearson (eds) *From Stonehenge to the Baltic: Living with cultural diversity in the third millennium BC,* 213–20. British Archaeological Reports International Series 1692. Oxford: Archaeopress.

Brück, J. 2005. Experiencing the past? The development of a phenomenological archaeology in British Prehistory. *Archaeological Dialogues* 12(1), 45–72.

Burenhult, G. 1980. *The Archaeological Excavation at Carrowmore, Co. Sligo, Ireland. Excavation Seasons 1977–9.* Stockholm: Stockholm University Institute of Archaeology.

Burenhult, G. 1984. *The Archaeology of Carrowmore. Environmental Archaeology and the Megalithic Tradition at Carrowmore, Co. Sligo, Ireland.* Stockholm: Stockholm University Theses and Papers in North-European Archaeology 14.

Burenhult, G. 2003. The chronology of Carrowmore. In G. Burenhult (ed.) *Stones and Bones: Formal disposal of the dead in Atlantic Europe during the Mesolithic Neolithic interface 6000–3000bc, Archaeological conference in honour of the late Professor Michael J. O'Kelly,* 66–9. Oxford: British Archaeological Reports, International Series 1201.

Burenhult, G. 2005. Carrowmore – tombs for hunters. *British Archaeology* 82, 22–7.

Burenhult, G. 2009. *The Illustrated Guide to the Megalithic Cemetery of Carrowmore Co. Sligo, Ireland,* 3rd edition. Tjörnarp, Sweden: Published by G. Burenhult.

Burrow, S. 2010. Bryn Celli Ddu passage tomb, Anglesey: alignment, construction, date and ritual. *Proceedings of the Prehistoric Society* 76, 249–270.

Card, N and Thomas, A. 2012. Painting a picture of Neolithic Orkney:

decorated stonework from the Ness of Brodgar. In A. Cochrane and A. Jones (eds) *Visualising the Neolithic: abstraction, figuration, performance, representation. Neolithic Studies Group Seminar Papers 13*, 112–124. Oxford: Oxbow Books.

Carlin, N. Forthcoming. Getting into the groove: exploring the relationship between Grooved Ware and developed passage tombs in Ireland *c.* 3000–2700 BC. *Proceedings of the Prehistoric Society.*

Cassen, S. 2000. Stelae reused in the passage graves of western France: history of research and a sexualisation of the carvings. In A. Ritchie (ed.) *Neolithic Orkney in its European Context*, 233–46. Cambridge: McDonald Institute for Archaeological Research.

Cassen, S. 2005. Pigeon-Raven, Snake and Sperm whale, magical objects and domestic horned. The division of the world during the early neo-Neolithic of western France. *Documenta Prehistorica* XXXIII, 197–204.

Cassen, S. 2009. *Exercice de stèle. Une archéologie des pierres dressées. Réflexions autour des menhirs de Carnac.* Paris: Errance.

Caulfield, S. 1983. The Neolithic settlement of North Connaught. In T. Reeves-Smyth and F. Hamond (eds) *Landscape archaeology in Ireland*, 195–216. Oxford: British Archaeological Reports British Series 116.

Challands, A., Muir, T. and Richards, C. 2005. The Great Passage Grave of Maeshowe. In C. Richards (ed.) *Dwelling among the monuments*, 229–48. Cambridge: McDonald Institute for Archaeological Research.

Childe, V. G. 1940. *Prehistoric Communities of the British Isles.* London: Chambers and Chambers.

Cochrane, A. 2009. Additive subtraction: addressing pick-dressing in Irish passage tombs. In J. Thomas and V. Oliveira Jorge (eds) *Archaeology and the politics of vision in a post-modern context*, 163–85. Cambridge: Cambridge Scholars Publishing.

Cody, E. 1987. Giant's Grave, Magheracar. In I. Bennett (ed.) *Excavations 1986: Summary Accounts of Archaeological Excavations in Ireland,* 15. Dublin: Wordwell.

Cody, E. 1988. Giant's Grave, Magheracar. In I. Bennett (ed.) *Excavations 1987: Summary Accounts of Archaeological Excavations in Ireland,* 12. Dublin: Wordwell.

Coffey, G. 1898. On a cairn excavated by Thomas Plunkett on Belmore Mountain, Co. Fermanagh. *Proceedings of the Royal Irish Academy* 20, 259–66.

Collins, A. and Waterman, D. 1955. *Millin Bay, a Late Neolithic Cairn in Co. Down.* Belfast: HMSO.

Condit, T. 1997. The Newgrange cursus and the theatre of ritual. *Archaeology Ireland* 34, 16–18.

Conwell, E. A. 1866. Examination of the ancient sepulchral cairns on the Loughcrew Hills, County of Meath. *Proceedings of the Royal Irish Academy (1st series)* 9, 355–79.

Conwell, E. A. 1873. *Discovery of the tomb of Ollamh Fodhla*. Dublin: McGlashan and Gill.

Cook. T. A. 1914. *The Curves of Life*. Constable and Company: London.

Cooney, G. 2000. *Landscapes of Neolithic Ireland*. London: Routledge.

Cooney, G. 2006. Newgrange – a view from the platform. *Antiquity* 80(309), 697–710.

Cooney, G., Bayliss, A., Healy, F., Whittle, A., Danaher, E., Cagney, L., Mallory, J., Smyth, J., Kador, T. and O'Sullivan, M. 2011. Ireland. In A. Whittle, F. Healy and A. Bayliss (eds) *Gathering Time. Dating the Early Neolithic Enclosures of Southern Britain and Ireland. Volume 2*, 562–669. Oxbow: Oxford.

Corlett, C. 2014. Some cursus monuments in South Leinster. *Archaeology Ireland* 28(2), 20–25.

Curran-Mulligan, P. 1994. Yes, but is it art! *Archaeology Ireland* 8(1), 14–15.

Danaher, K. 1972. *The Year in Ireland*. Dublin: Mercier Press.

Daniel, G. 1950. *The Prehistoric Chamber Tombs of England and Wales*. Cambridge: Cambridge University Press.

Dark, P. and Gent, H. 2001. Pests and diseases of prehistoric crops: a yield 'honeymoon' for early grain crops in Europe? *Oxford Journal of Archaeology* 20(1), 59–78.

Davies, P. and Robb, J. 2004. Scratches in the earth: the underworld as a theme in British prehistory, with particular reference to the Neolithic and Earlier Bronze Age. *Landscape Research* 29(2), 141–51

Dehn, T. and Hansen, S. I. 2006. Architecture Mégalithique en Scandinavie. In R. Joussaume, L. Laporte and C. Scarre (eds) *Origine et développement du mégalithisme de l'ouest de l'Europe*, 39–62. Bougon: Musée de Bougon.

Devereux, P. and Jahn, R. G. 1996. Acoustical Resonances of Selected Sites. *Antiquity* 70(268), 665–6.

Dietler, M. 2011. Feasting and Fasting. In Timothy Insoll (ed.) *The Oxford Handbook of the Archaeology of Ritual and Religion*, 179–94. Oxford: Oxford University Press.

Dronfield, J. 1995a. Migraine, light, and hallucinogens: the neurocognitive basis of Irish megalithic art. *Oxford Journal of Archaeology* 14, 261–75.

Dronfield, J. 1995b. Subjective vision and the source of Irish megalithic art. *Antiquity* 69, 539–49.

Dronfield, J. 1996a. Entering alternative realities: cognition, art and architecture in Irish passage-tombs. *Cambridge Archaeological Journal* 6, 37–72.

Dronfield, J. 1996b. The vision thing: diagnosis of endogenous derivation in abstract arts. *Current Anthropology* 37(2), 373–91.

Eliade, M. 1956. *The forge and the crucible*. Chicago: University of Chicago Press.

Eliasson, O. 1997. *Your Sun Machine*. Los Angeles: Marc Foxx Gallery.

Eliasson, O. 2003. *The Weather Project*. The Unilever Series 2003: Tate Modern

Eliot, T. S. 1921. *The sacred wood: Essays on Poetry and Criticism*. New York: Alfred A. Knopf.

Eogan, G. 1979. Objects with Iberian affinities from Knowth. *Revista de Gumaraes* 89, 275–80.

Eogan, G. 1982. Two maceheads from Knowth, Co. Meath. *Journal of the Royal Society of Antiquaries of Ireland* 112, 123–38.

Eogan, G. 1984. *Excavations at Knowth 1: Smaller passage tombs, Neolithic occupation and Beaker activity*. Dublin: Royal Irish Academy, Monographs in Archaeology.

Eogan, G. 1986. *Knowth and the passage tombs of Ireland*. London: Thames and Hudson.

Eogan, G. 1990. Irish megalithic tombs and Iberia: comparisons and contrasts. In *Probleme der Megalithgraberforschung*, 113–38. Madrid: Deutsches archäologisches Institut.

Eogan, G. 1992. Scottish and Irish passage tombs: some comparisons and contrasts. In N. Sharpies and A. Sheridan (eds) *Vessels for the ancestors. Essays on the Neolithic of Britain and Ireland*, 120–7. Edinburgh: Edinburgh University Press.

Eogan, G. 1997. Overlays and underlays: aspects of megalithic art succession at Brugh na Bóinne, Ireland. *Brigantium* 10, 217–34.

Eogan, G. 1998. Knowth before Knowth. *Antiquity* 72, 162–72.

Eogan, G. 1999. Megalithic art and society. *Proceedings of the Prehistoric Society* 65, 415–46.

Eogan, G. 2006. The Irish megalithic tombs in their social settings. In R. Joussame, L. Laporte and C. Scarre (eds) *Origin and development of the megalithic monuments of western Europe (Bougon-26/30 October 2002)*, 135–57. Bougon: Musée des Tumulus de Bougon.

Eogan, G. 2009. Dowth passage tomb: note on possible structural sequence. *Ríocht na Midhe* 20, 1–4.

Eogan, G. with Doyle, P. 2010. *Guide to the passage tombs at Brú na Bóinne*. Revealing Heritage Series. Dublin: Wordwell

Eogan, G. with Cleary, K. Forthcoming. *Excavations at Knowth 6: The Great Mound at Knowth (Tomb 1) and its passage tomb archaeology*. Dublin: Royal Irish Academy.

Ereira, A. 2009. *The Elder Brothers' Warning*. London: Tairona Heritage Trust.

Eriksen, P. 2006. The rolling stones of Newgrange. *Antiquity* 80, 709–10.

Eriksen, P. 2008. The Great Mound of Newgrange. *Acta Archaeologica* 79(1), 250–73.

Fergusson, J. 1872. *Rude stone monuments in all countries: their age and uses*. London: John Murray.

Fowler, C. and Cummings, V. 2003. Places of transformation: building monuments from water and stone in the Neolithic of the Irish Sea. *Journal of the Royal Anthropological Institute* 9, 1–20.

Francfort, H-P. & Hamayon, R. N. in collaboration with Bahn, P. G. (eds) 2003. *The Concept of shamanism, Uses and Abuses*. Bibliotheca Shamanistica 10. Budapest: Akacdemiai Kiado.

Fraser, R. A., Bogaard, A., Heaton, T., Charles, M., Jones, G., Christensen, B. T., Halstead, P., Merbach, I., Poulton, P. R., Sparkes, D. and Styring, A. 2011. Manuring and stable nitrogen isotope ratios in cereals and pulses: towards a new archaeobotanical approach to the inference of land use and dietary practices. *Journal of Archaeological Science* 38, 2790–804.

Fraser, S. M. 1998. The public forum and the space between: the materiality of social strategy in the Irish Neolithic. *Proceedings of the Prehistoric Society* 64, 203–44.

Ghilardi, B. and O'Connell, M. 2013a. Fine-resolution pollen-analytical study of Holocene woodland dynamics and land use in north Sligo, Ireland. *Boreas,* 42(3), 623.

Ghilardi, B. and O'Connell, M. 2013b. Early Holocene vegetation and climate dynamics with particular reference to the 8.2 ka event: pollen and macrofossil evidence from a small lake in western Ireland. *Vegetation History and Archaeobotany,* 22(2), 99–114.

Ghilardi, B. and O'Connell, M. 2013c. Prehistoric farming at Lough Dargan, north Sligo and its impact on the terrestrial environment. In Timoney, M. A. (ed.) *Dedicated to Sligo. Thirty-four essays on Sligo's past*, 15–28. Keash: Tasks.

Goldman, I. 1975. *The Mouth of Heaven: Introduction to Kwakiutl Religious Thought*. New York and London: John Wiley & Sons Inc.

Greenhalgh, M. 2005. *Atlantic Salmon: An Illustrated Natural History*. Ludlow: Merlin Unwin books.

Harbison, P. 1988. *Pre-Christian Ireland*. London: Thames and Hudson.

Harbison, P. 2003. *Treasures of the Boyne Valley*. Dublin: Gill & Macmillan.

Hartnett, P. J. 1957. Excavation of a passage grave at Fourknocks, Co. Meath. *Proceedings of the Royal Irish Academy* 58C, 197–277.

Hartnett, P. J. 1971. The excavation of two tumuli at Fourknocks (Sites II and III), Co. Meath. *Proceedings of the Royal Irish Academy* 71C, 35–83.

Hemp, W. J. 1930. The chambered cairn of Bryn Celli Ddu. *Archaeologia Serliana* 2(80), 179–214.

Hemp. W. J. 1936. The chambered cairn known as Bryn yr Hen Bobl near Plas Newydd, Anglesey. *Archaeologia* 85, 253–92.

Hensey, R. 2008. The observance of light: a ritualistic perspective on 'imperfect' alignments. *Time and Mind* 1(3), 319–30.

Hensey, R. 2010. *Ritual and belief in the passage tomb tradition of Ireland*. Unpublished PhD thesis submitted to the National University of Ireland, Galway.

Hensey, R. 2012. Assuming the Jigsaw had only one piece: abstraction, figuration and the interpretation of Irish passage tomb art. In A. Jones and A. Cochrane (eds) *Visualising the Neolithic: abstraction, figuration, performance, representation. Neolithic Studies Group Seminar Papers 13*, 161–78. Oxford: Oxbow Books.

Hensey, R. 2014. Artefact versus architecture: the use and interpretation of space within Irish passage tombs. In G. Robin, A. D'Anna, A. Schmitt and M. Bailly (eds) Functions, uses and representations of space in the monumental tombs of the European Neolithic. *Préhistoires Méditerranéennes*.

Hensey, R. and Bergh, S. 2013. 'The inns at Sligo are better than those at Auray... and the scenery far more beautiful': Carrowmore re-visited. In M. A. Timoney (ed.) *Publishing Sligo's Past: Dedicated to Sligo,* 41–3. Tasks: Keash, Sligo.

Hensey, R., Meehan, P., Dowd, M. and Moore S. 2014. A century of archaeology – historical excavation and modern research at the Carrowkeel passage tombs, County Sligo. *Proceedings of the Royal Irish Academy*, Section C, 114, 57–86.

Hensey, R. and Robin, G. 2011. More than meets the eye: new recordings of megalithic art in North-West Ireland. *Oxford Journal of Archaeology* 30(2), 109–30.

Hensey, R. and Robin, G. 2012. Once upon a time in the West: the first discoveries of art in the Carrowkeel-Keashcorran passage tomb complex, Co. Sligo. *Archaeology Ireland*, 23(3), 26–9.

Herity, M. 1974. *Irish Passage Graves: Neolithic tomb-builders in Ireland and Britain, 2500 BC*. Dublin: Irish University Press.

Herity, M. and Eogan, G. 1977. *Ireland in Prehistory*. London: Routledge & Kegan Paul.

Hugh-Jones, S. 1996. Shamans, Prophets, Priests and Pastors. In N. Thomas and C. Humphrey (eds) *Shamanism, History & the State*, 32–75. Ann Arbor: University of Michigan Press.

Humphrey, C. 1995. Chiefly and shamanistic landscapes in Mongolia. In E. Hirsch and M. O'Hanlon (eds) *The Anthropology of landscape: perspectives on place and space*, 135–62. Oxford: Clarendon Press.

Ingold, T. 2000. *The perception of the environment: essays in livelihood, dwelling and skill*. London: Routledge.

Iteanu, A. 1990. The concept of the person and the ritual system: an Orokaiva view. *Man* 25, 35–53.

Jones, A. 1999. Local Colour: Megalithic Architecture and Colour Symbolism in Neolithic Arran. *Oxford Journal of Archaeology* 18(4), 339–50.

Jones, A. 2004. By way of illustration: art, memory and materiality in the Irish Sea and beyond. In V. Cummings and C. Fowler (eds) *The Neolithic of the Irish Sea: materiality and traditions of practice*, 202–13. Oxford: Oxbow.

Jones, A. and MacGregor, G. (eds) 2002. *Colouring the Past*. Oxford: Berg.

Jones, A. and Richards, C. 2003. Animals into ancestors: domestification, food and identity in Late Neolithic Orkney. In M. Parker Pearson (ed.) BAR International Series 117, *Food, Culture and Identity in the Neolithic and Early Bronze Age*, 45–52. Oxford: Archaeopress.

Jones, C. 2007. *Temples of stone – exploring the megalithic tombs of Ireland*. Cork: The Collins Press.

Kador, T., Geber, J., Hensey, R., Meehan. P. and Moore, S. Forthcoming. New dates from Carrowkeel. *Past*.

Kehoe, Alice B. 2000. *Shamans and religion: an anthropological exploration in critical thinking*. Long Grove: Waveland Press, Inc.

L'Helgouach, J. 1965. *Les sépultures mégalithiques en Armorique*. Rennes: Travaux du Laboratoire d'Anthropologie Préhistorique de la Faculté des Sciences.

Lewis-Williams, J. D. and Dowson, T. A. 1993. On vision and power in the Neolithic: evidence from the decorated monuments. *Current Anthropology* 34(1), 55–65.

Lewis-Williams, J. D. and Pearce, D. 2005. *Inside the Neolithic mind:*

Consciousness, Cosmos and the Realm of the Gods. London: Thames and Hudson.

Lynch, A. 2014. Poulnabrone: An early Neolithic portal tomb in Ireland. Bray: Wordwell

Lynch, A. Forthcoming. Newgrange revisited: new insights from excavations at the back of the mound in 1984–1988. *Journal of Irish Archaeology*.

Lynch, F. M. 1969. The megalithic tombs of North Wales. In T. G. E. Powell, J. X. P. W. Corcoran, F. M. Lynch and J. C. Scott (eds) *Megalithic enquiries in the West of Britain*, 107–74. Liverpool: University of Liverpool Press.

Lynch, F. M. 1975. Excavations at Carreg Samson, Mathry, Pembrokeshire. *Archaeologia Cambrensis* 124, 15–35

Lynch, F. M. 1998. Colour in prehistoric architecture. In A. Gibson and D. D. A. Simpson (eds) *Prehistoric ritual and religion: essays in honour of Aubrey Burl*, 62–7. Stroud: Sutton Publishing.

Lynch, F. M. 2000. The earlier Neolithic. In F. M. Lynch, S. Aldhouse-Green and J. L. Davies, *Prehistoric Wales*, 42–78. Stroud: Tempus.

Macalister, R. A. S. 1932. A burial cairn on Seefin Mountain, Co. Wicklow. *Journal of the Royal Society of Antiquaries of Ireland* 62, 153–7.

Macalister, R. A. S., Armstrong, E. and Praeger, R. 1912. Report on the exploration of Bronze-Age Carns on Carrowkeel Mountain, Co. Sligo. *Proceedings of the Royal Irish Academy* 29C, 311–47.

MacKie, E. 1997. Maeshowe and the winter solstice: ceremonial aspects of the Orkney Grooved Ware culture. *Antiquity* 71(272), 338–59.

May, S. 2003. Meteorologica. In S. Mays (ed.) *Olafur Eliasson: The Weather Project. Exhibition catalogue*, 15–28. London: Tate Publishing.

McClatchie, M., Bogaard, A., Colledge, S., Whitehouse, N. J., Schulting, R. J., Barratt, P. and McLaughlin, T. R. 2014. Neolithic farming in north-western Europe: archaeobotanical evidence from Ireland. *Journal of Archaeological Science*, 51, 206–15.

McCormick, F. 1986. Animal bones from prehistoric Irish burials. *Journal of Irish Archaeology* 3, 37–48.

McGuinness, D. 1995. The passage tombs of Co. Dublin: a note on previous accounts. *Trowel* VI, 5–11.

McMann, J. 1993. *Loughcrew: the cairns. A guide to an ancient Irish landscape*. Oldcastle: After Hours Books.

McMann, J. 1994. Forms of power: dimensions of an Irish megalithic landscape. *Antiquity* 68, 525–44.

McSparron, C. 2008. Have you no homes to go to: calling time on the early Irish Neolithic. *Archaeology Ireland* 22(3), 18–21.

Meehan, P. 2012. A possible astronomical alignment marking seasonal transitions at Listoghil, Sligo, Ireland. *Internet Archaeology* 32.

Meighan, I., Simpson, D. A. A. and Hartwell, B. 2002. Newgrange – sourcing of its granitic cobbles. *Archaeology Ireland* 16(1), 32–5.

Meighan, I., Simpson, D. A. A., Hartwell, B. N., Fallick, A. E. and Kennan, P. S. 2003. Sourcing the quartz at Newgrange, Brú na Bóinne, Ireland. In G. Burenhult (ed.) *Stones and bones: formal disposal of the dead in Atlantic Europe during the Mesolithic-Neolithic interface 6000–3000 BC. Archaeological conference in honour of the late professor Michael J. O'Kelly*, 247–51. BAR International Series 1201. Oxford: Archaeopress.

Meryman, R. 1965. Interview with Andrew Wyeth. *Life Magazine* 14, 93–114.

Mills A. and Slobodin, R. 1994. *Amerindian rebirth: reincarnation belief among North American Indians and Inuit*. Toronto: University of Toronto Press.

Mitchell, G. F. 1984. The landscape. In G. Eogan, *Excavations at Knowth 1*. Dublin: Royal Irish Academy, 9–11.

Mitchell, G. F. 1992. Notes on some non-local cobbles at the entrances to the passage-graves at Newgrange and Knowth, Co. Meath. *Journal of the Royal Society of Antiquaries of Ireland* 122, 128–45.

Mitchell, G. F. 1995. Did the tide once flow as far as Newgrange? *Living Heritage* 12, 128–45.

Mooney, J. 1896. The Ghost-Dance Religion and the Sioux Outbreak of 1890. *Fourteenth annual Report of the bureau of American Ethnology to the Secretary of the Smithsonian Institution*, 1892–3. Part 2.

Moroney, A. M. 1999. *Dowth: Winter Sunsets*. Drogheda: Flax Mill Publications.

Newman, C. 1995. A Cursus at Loughcrew, Co. Meath. *Archaeology Ireland* 9(4), 19–21.

Newman, C. 1999. Notes on Four Cursus-like monuments in Co. Meath, Ireland. In A. Barclay and J. Harding (eds) *Pathways and ceremonies: the Cursus Monuments of Neolithic Britain and Ireland*, 141–47. Oxford: Oxford Archaeological Unit.

O'Connell, M., Ghilardi, B. and Morrison, L. 2014. A 7000–year record of environmental change, including early farming impact, based on lake-sediment geochemistry and pollen data from County Sligo, western Ireland. *Quaternary Research* 81**,** 35–49.

Ó hÓgáin, D. 1999. *The Sacred Isle – Belief and Religion in Pre-Christian Ireland*. Cork: The Collins Press.

O'Kelly, C. 1973. Passage-grave art in the Boyne Valley. *Proceedings of the Prehistoric Society* 39, 354–82.

O'Kelly, C. 1978. *Illustrated guide to Newgrange and the other Boyne Monuments,* 3rd edition. Cork: Published by the author.

O'Kelly, C. 1982. Corpus of Newgrange art. In M. J. O'Kelly, *Newgrange: archaeology, art and legend,* 146–85. London: Thames and Hudson.

O'Kelly, M. J. 1964. Newgrange, Co. Meath. *Antiquity* 38, 288–90.

O'Kelly, M. J. 1973. Current excavations at Newgrange, Ireland. In G. Daniel and P. Kjærum (eds), *Megalithic graves and ritual: papers presented at the III Atlantic colloquium, Moesgård* 1969, 137–46. Copenhagen: Jutland Archaeological Society.

O'Kelly, M. J. 1979. The restoration of Newgrange. *Antiquity* 53, 205–10.

O'Kelly, M. J. 1982. *Newgrange, Archaeology, Art and Legend.* London: Thames and Hudson.

O'Kelly, M. J., Lynch, F. and O'Kelly, C. 1978. Three passage graves at Newgrange, Co. Meath. *Proceedings of the Royal Irish Academy* 78C, 249–352.

O'Kelly, M. J. and O'Kelly, C. 1983. The tumulus of Dowth, Co. Meath. *Proceedings of the Royal Irish Academy* 83C, 136–90.

O'Neill, J. 2013. Being Prehistoric in the Irish Iron Age. In M. O'Sullivan, C. Scarre, and M. Doyle (eds) *Tara – from the Past to the Future,* 256–66. Dublin: Wordwell.

Ó Nualláin, S. 1968. A ruined megalithic cemetery in Co. Donegal and its context in the Irish passage grave series. *Journal of the Royal Society of Antiquaries of Ireland* 98, 1–29.

Ó Ríordáin, S. P. and Daniel, G. 1964. *Newgrange and the Bend of the Boyne.* London: Thames and Hudson.

O'Sullivan, M. 1986. Approaches to passage tomb art. *Journal of the Royal Society of Antiquaries of Ireland* 116, 68–83.

O'Sullivan, M. 1989. A stylistic revolution in the megalithic art of the Boyne Valley. *Archaeology Ireland* 3(4), 138–42.

O'Sullivan, M. 1993a. *Megalithic art in Ireland.* Dublin: Town House and Country House.

O'Sullivan, M. 1993b. Recent investigations at Knockroe passage tomb. *Journal of the Royal Society of Antiquaries of Ireland* 123, 5–18.

O'Sullivan, M. 1995. The east tomb at Knockroe. *Old Kilkenny Review* 47, 11–30.

O'Sullivan, M. 1996a. A platform to the past – Knockroe passage tomb. *Archaeology Ireland* 10(2), 11–13.

O'Sullivan, M. 1996b. Comment on 'Entering alternative realities: cognition, art and architecture in Irish Passage Tombs' by J. Dronfield. *Cambridge Archaeological Journal* 6(1), 59.

O'Sullivan, M. 1997. Megalithic art in Ireland and Brittany: divergence or convergence. In J. L'Helgouac'h, C. Le Roux and J. Lecornec (eds) *Art et symboles du mégalithisme Européen. Actes du 2ème Colloque International sur l'art mégalithique, Nantes, juin 1995. Revue archéologique de l'Ouest, Supplément no. 8*, 81–96. Nantes.

O'Sullivan, M. 2004. Little and Large: Comparing Knockroe with Knowth. In H. Roche, E. Grogan, J. Bradley, J. Coles and B. Raftery (eds) *From Megaliths to Metal: Essays in Honour of George Eogan*, 44–50. Oxford: Oxbow.

O'Sullivan, M. 2005. *Duma na nGiall: the Mound of the Hostages, Tara.* Bray: Wordwell in association with the UCD, school of Archaeology.

O'Sullivan, M. 2006. The Boyne and beyond: a review of megalithic art in Ireland. In R. Joussaume, L. Laporte and C. Scarre (eds) *Origine et développement du mégalithisme de l'ouest de l'Europe. Actes du colloque international, 26–30 octobre 2002, Bougon (France), Niort: Conseil Général des Deux-Sèvres*, 2 vols, 649–86. Bougon.

Patrick, J. 1974. Midwinter sunrise at Newgrange. *Nature* 249, 517–19.

Patton, M. 1990. On entoptic images in context: art, monuments, and society in Neolithic Brittany. *Current Anthropology* 31(5), 554–8.

Patton M., Rodwell, W. and Finch, O. 1999. *La Hougue Bie, Jersey, a study of the Neolithic Tomb, Medieval chapels and Prince's Tower, including a report on the 1991–1994 excavation.* Jersey: Société Jersiaise.

Petrie, G. 1838. An account of a very remarkable collection of stone circles, cairns, etc., situate in the townland of Carrowmore. *Proceedings of the Royal Irish Academy* 1, 140–2.

Phillips, A., Corcoran, M. and Eogan, G. 2001. *Derivation of the source localities for the kerb, orthostat and standing stones of the Neolithic passage graves of the Boyne Valley, Co. Meath.* Unpublished report for the Heritage Council. Department of Geology, Trinity College Dublin.

Phillips, A., Corcoran, M. and Eogan, G. 2002. *Identification of the source area for megaliths used in the construction of the Neolithic passage graves of the Boyne Valley, Co. Meath.* Unpublished report for the Heritage Council. Department of Geology, Trinity College Dublin.

Piggott, S. 1954. *The Neolithic Cultures of the British Isles.* Cambridge: Cambridge University Press.

Powell, A. B. 1994. Newgrange – Science or Symbolism. *Proceedings of the Prehistoric Society* 60, 85–96.

Powell, T. and Daniel, G. 1956. *Barclodiad y Gawres: the excavation of a megalithic chamber tomb in Anglesey 1952–1953.* Liverpool: Liverpool University Press.

Prendergast, F. 2009. *Passage Tomb X1, Patrickstown, Co. Meath – a report of new passage tomb art and a potential alignment of the passage on the winter solstice sunset*. Report to the National Monuments Service, Department of the Environment, Heritage and Local Government.

Prendergast, F. 2011a. *Linked Landscapes: Spatial, Archaeoastronomical and Social Network Analysis of the Irish Passage Tomb Tradition*. Unpublished PhD thesis submitted to University College Dublin.

Prendergast, F. 2011b. The Loughcrew Hills and Passage Tomb Complex. In B. Stefanini and G. M. Glynn (eds) *Field Guide No. 29 – North Meath*, 42–54. Dublin: Irish Quaternary Association.

Quinn, T. P., Stewart, I. J. and Boatright, C. P. 2006. Experimental evidence of homing to site of incubation by mature sockeye salmon, *Oncorhynchus nerka*. *Animal Behaviour* 72, 941–9.

Radford, C. A. R. 1958. The chambered tomb at Broadsands, Paignton, *Proceedings of the Devon Archaeological Exploration Society* 5(5–6), 147–167.

Raftery, J. 2009. Newtown, Loughcrew, Oldcastle, County Meath. Cairn H, August 5–November 10, 1943. In G. Cooney, K. Becker, J. Coles, M. Ryan and S. Sievers (eds) *Relics of old decency: archaeological studies in later prehistory. Festschrift for Barry Raftery*, 531–42. Dublin: Wordwell.

Ramírez, P. R., Behrmann, R de B., Laporte, L., Gouézin, P., Cousseau, F., Bermejo, R. B., Gismero, A. H., Cela, M. I. and Quesnel, L. 2015. Natural and artificial colours: the megalithic monuments of Brittany. Antiquity 89, 55–71. doi:10.15184/aqy.2014.29

Ray, T. 1989. The winter solstice phenomenon at Newgrange, Ireland: accident or design? *Nature* 337, 343–5.

Renfrew, C. 1973. *Before Civilisation: The Radiocarbon Revolution and Prehistoric Europe*. London: Cape.

Renfrew, C. 1984. *Approaches to Social Archaeology*. Edinburgh: Edinburgh University Press.

Richards, C. 1996. Monuments as landscape: creating the centre of the world in Late Neolithic Orkney. *World Archaeology* 28(2), 190–208.

Ritchie, J. N. G. 1970. Excavation of the chambered cairn at Achnacreebeag. *Proceedings of the Society of Antiquaries of Scotland* 102 (1969–1970), 31–55.

Richards, M. P., Schulting, R. J., and Hedges, R. E. M. 2003. Sharp shift in diet at onset of Neolithic. *Nature* 425, 366.

Robb, J. 2001. Island identities: ritual, travel and the creation of difference in Neolithic Malta. European Journal of Archaeology 4(2), 175–202.

Roberts, C. 2007. *The unnatural history of the sea: the past and future of humanity and fishing*. London: Island Press.

Robin, G. 2008. *Neolithic passage tomb art around the Irish Sea Iconography and spatial organisation*. Ph.D. Thesis submitted to the University of Nantes.

Robin, G. 2009. *L'architecture des signes: l'art parietal des tombeaux néolithiques autour de la mer d'Irlande*. Collection Archéologie et Culture. Rennes. Presses Universitaires de Rennes.

Robin, G. 2010. Spatial structures and symbolic systems in Irish and British passing tombs: the architectural organization of the elements, parietal carved signs and funerary deposits. *Cambridge Archaeological Journal* 20 3), 373–418.

Robin, G. 2012. The figurative part of an abstract Neolithic iconography: hypotheses and directions of research in Irish and British passage tomb art. In A. Jones and A. Cochrane (eds) *Visualising the Neolithic: abstraction, figuration, performance, representation. Neolithic Studies Group Seminar Papers 13*, 140–60. Oxford: Oxbow.

Roche, J. and McHutchison, M. (eds) 1998. *First fish, first people: Salmon tales of the North Pacific rim*. Seattle: University of Washington Press.

Rotherham, E. 1895. On the excavation of a cairn on Slieve-na-Caillighe, Loughcrew. *Journal of the Royal Society of Antiquaries* 25, 311–16.

Roy, J. 1986. Interview with M. J. O'Kelly in *The Road wet the wind close*, 33–44. Dublin: Gill and Macmillan.

Ruggles, C. L. N. 1999. *Astronomy in Prehistoric Britain and Ireland*. New Haven: Yale University Press.

Ruggles, C. L. N. and Saunders, N. J. 1993. The Study of Cultural Astronomy. In C. L. N. Ruggles and N. J. Saunders (eds) *Astronomies and Cultures: Papers derived from the third 'Oxford' International Symposium on archaeoastronomy, St. Andrews, UK, September 1990*, 1–32. Colorado: University Press of Colorado.

Rynne, E. 1960. Survey of a probable passage grave cemetery at Bremore, Co. Dublin. *Journal of the Royal Society of Antiquaries of Ireland* 60, 79–81.

Scarre, C. 1998. Traditions of death: mounded tombs, megalithic art, and funerary ideology in Neolithic Western Europe. In M. Edmonds and C. Richards (eds) *Understanding the Neolithic of North-Western Europe*, 161–87. Glasgow: Cruithne Press.

Scarre, C. 2011. *Landscapes of Neolithic Brittany*. Oxford: Oxford University Press.

Scarre, C. and Lawson, G. (eds) 2006. *Archaeoacoustics*. Cambridge: McDonald Institute for Archaeological Research, University of Cambridge.

Schulting, R. J. 2013. On the northwestern fringes: Earlier Neolithic subsistence in Britain and Ireland as seen through faunal remains and stable isotopes. In S. Colledge, J. Conolly, K. Dobney, K. Manning and S.

Shennan (eds) *The Origins and Spread of Stock-Keeping in the Near East and Europe*, 313–38. Walnut Creek, California: Left Coast Press.

Schulting, R. J. and Richards, M. P. 2002. The wet, the wild and the domesticated: the Mesolithic-Neolithic transition on the west coast of Scotland. *European Journal of Archaeology* 5, 147–89.

Schwimmer, E. 1973. *Exchange in the social structure of the Orokaiva: traditional and emergent ideologies in the Northern District of Papua*. London: Hurst.

Shee, E. 1973. Techniques of Irish passage grave art. In G. Daniel and P. Kjærum (eds) *Megalithic graves and ritual: papers presented at the III Atlantic colloquium, Moesgård 1969*, 163–72. Copenhagen: Jutland Archaeological Society.

Shee Twohig, E. 1981. *The megalithic art of western Europe*. Oxford: Clarendon Press.

Shee Twohig, E. 1995. An inter-tidal passage tomb at 'The Lag', Ringarogy Island, Co. Cork. *Archaeology Ireland* 9(4), 7–9.

Shee Twohig, E. 2000. Frameworks for the megalithic art of the Boyne Valley. In A. Desmond, G. Johnston, M. McCarthy, J. Sheehan and E. Shee Twohig (eds) *New agendas in Irish prehistory: papers in commemoration of Liz Anderson*, 89–105. Bray: Wordwell.

Shee Twohig, E. 2004. *Irish megalithic tombs*. 2nd edition. Princes Risborough: Shire Books.

Shee Twohig, E., Roughley, C., Shell, C., O'Reilly, C., Clarke, P. and Swanton, G. 2010. Open-air rock art at Loughcrew, Co. Meath. *Journal of Irish Archaeology,* Volume XIX, 1–28.

Sheridan, A. 1986. Megaliths and megalomania: an account, and interpretation, of the development of passage tombs in Ireland. *The Journal of Irish Archaeology* 3, 17–30.

Sheridan, J. A. 2000. Achnacreebeag and its French connections: vive the 'auld alliance'. In J. C. Henderson (ed.) *The prehistory and early history of Atlantic Europe: papers from a session held at the European association of archaeologists fourth annual meeting in Göteborg 1998*, 1–15. Oxford: British Archaeological Reports, International Series 861.

Sheridan, J. A. 2003a. French connections I: spreading the marmites thinly. In I. Armit, E. Murphy, E. Nelis and D. A. A. Simpson (eds) *Neolithic settlement in Ireland and western Britain*, 3–17. Oxford: Oxbow Books.

Sheridan, J. A. 2003b. Ireland's earliest 'passage' tombs: a French connection. In G. Burenhult (ed.) *Stones and bones: formal disposal of the dead in Atlantic Europe during the Mesolithic–Neolithic interface 6000–3000 BC. Archaeological conference in honour of the late professor Michael J. O'Kelly*, 9–25. Oxford: BAR International Series 1201.

Sheridan, J. A. 2003c. The chronology of Irish megalithic tombs. In G. Burenhult (ed.) *Stones and bones: formal disposal of the dead in Atlantic Europe during the Mesolithic-Neolithic interface 6000–3000 BC. Archaeological conference in honour of the late professor Michael J. O'Kelly*, 69–73. Oxford: BAR International Series 1201.

Sheridan, J. A. 2010. The Neolithization of Britain and Ireland: the 'Big Picture'. In B. Finlayson and G. Warren (eds), *Landscapes in Transition*, 89–105. Oxford: Oxbow.

Sheridan, J. A., Schulting, R., Quinnell, H. and Taylor, R. 2008. *Revisiting a small passage tomb at Broadsands, Devon*. Proceedings of the Devon Archaeological Society 66, 1–26.

Simpson, D. D. A. 1988. The stone maceheads of Ireland. *Journal of the Royal Society of Antiquaries of Ireland* 118, 27–52.

Smith, C. A. and Lynch, F. M. 1987. *Trefignath and Din Dryfol: The Excavation of Two Megalithic Tombs in Anglesey*. Cardiff: Cambrian Archaeological Association, Monograph 3.

Smyth, J. (ed.) 2009. *Brú na Bóinne World Heritage Site Research Framework*. Dublin: The Heritage Council.

Smyth, J. 2014. *Settlement in Neolithic Ireland: new discoveries on the edge of Europe, Prehistoric Society Research Paper 6*. Oxford: Prehistoric Society.

Stoddart, S., Bonanno, A., Gouder, T., Malone, C. and Trump, D. 1993. Cult in an island Society: prehistoric Malta in the Tarxien period. *Cambridge Archaeological Journal* 3, 3–19.

Stolze, S. 2012a. High-resolution palaeoecological data from the Carrowkeel area, western Ireland: Landscape change and human settlement dynamics during the fourth millennium BC. *Quaternary International* 279–280, 470.

Stolze, S. 2012b. Environmental change and human impact during the Neolithic in the Carrowkeel-Keshcorran area: Evidence from Lough Availe, Roscommon and South Sligo. In S. Bettina and G. McGlynn, *Irish Quaternary Association, Field Guide No. 30, Roscommon and South Sligo*, 83–90. Dublin: Irish Quaternary Association.

Stolze, S., Dörfler, W., Monecke, T. and Nelle, O. 2012: Evidence for climatic variability and its impact on human development during the Neolithic from Loughmeenaghan, County Sligo, Ireland. *Journal of Quaternary Science* 27(4), 393–403.

Stolze, S. Dörfler, W. and Nelle, O. 2013a A high-resolution palaeoecological reconstruction of landscape change and human development during the fourth millennium BC in the Carrowkeel/Keshcorran area, Co. Sligo. In M. A. Timoney (ed.) *Dedicated to Sligo. Thirty-four essays on Sligo's past*, 29–36. Keash: Tasks.

Stolze, S., Muscheler, R., Dörfler, W. and Nelle, O. 2013b. Solar influence on climate variability and human development during the Neolithic: evidence from a high-resolution multi-proxy record from Templevanny Lough, County Sligo, Ireland. *Quaternary Science Reviews* 67, 138–59.

Stout, G. 2002. *Newgrange and the bend of the Boyne*. Cork: Cork University Press.

Stout G. 2010. Monumentality and inclusion in the Boyne Valley, County Meath, Ireland. In J. Leary, D. Field and T. Darvill (eds) *Round Mounds and Monumentality in the British Neolithic and Beyond*, Neolithic Studies Group Seminar Papers 10, 197–210. Oxford: Oxbow Books.

Stout, G. and Stout, M. 2008. *Newgrange*. Cork: Cork University Press.

Swann, W. B., Jensen, J., Gomez, A., Whitehouse, H. and Bastian, B. 2012. When group membership gets personal: A theory of identity fusion. *Psychological Review* 119, No. 3, 441–56.

Thomas, J. S. 1990. Monuments from the inside: the case of the Irish megalithic tombs. *World Archaeology* 22(2), 168–78.

Thomas, J. S. 1992. Monuments, movement and the context of megalithic art. In N. Sharples and A. Sheridan (eds) *Vessels for the ancestors*, 143–55. Edinburgh: Edinburgh University.

Thomas, J. S. 2003. Thoughts on the 'repacked' Neolithic revolution. *Antiquity* 77, 67–74.

Tilley, C. 1996. *An ethnography of the Neolithic: early prehistoric societies in southern Scandinavia*. Cambridge: Cambridge University Press.

Tilley, C. 2004. *The materiality of stone: explorations in landscape phenomenology 1*. Oxford: Berg.

Tilley, C. 2008. *Body and Image: Explorations in Landscape Phenomenology 2*. Walnut Creek, CA: Left Coast Press.

Turner, V. 1967. *The forest of symbols: aspects of Ndembu ritual*. Ithaca: Cornell University Press.

United Nations Report. 2007. *World Urbanization Prospects: The 2007 Revision*. Department of Economic and Social Affairs Population Division: New York.

Vallancey, C. 1786. Druidism revised: or, a dissertation on the characters and modes of writing used by the Irish. *Collectanea de Rebus Hibernicis* 2(7), 161–217.

Walshe, P. 1941. The excavation of a burial cairn on Baltinglass Hill, Co. Wicklow. *Proceedings of the Royal Irish Academy* 46C, 221–36.

Watson, A. 2001. The Sounds of Transformation: Acoustics, Monuments and Ritual in the British Neolithic. In N. Price (ed.) *The Archaeology of Shamanism*, 178–92. London: Routledge.

Watson, A. and Keating, D. 2000. The architecture of sound in Neolithic

Orkney. In A. Ritchie (ed.) *Neolithic Orkney in its European Context*, 259–63. Cambridge: McDonald Institute for Archaeological Research.

Whittle, A. 1996. *Europe in the Neolithic: the creation of new worlds*. Cambridge: Cambridge University Press.

Whittle, A. 2000. 'Very like a whale': menhirs, motifs and myths in the Mesolithic-Neolithic transition of northwest Europe. *Cambridge Archaeological Journal* 10(2), 243–59.

Whitehouse, H. 1996. Rites of terror: emotion, metaphor, and memory in Melanesian initiation cults. *Journal of the Royal Anthropological Institute* 2, 703–15.

Whitehouse, H. 2000. *Arguments and icons: divergent modes of religiosity*. Oxford: Oxford University Press.

Whitehouse, H. 2004. *Modes of religiosity: a cognitive theory of religious transmission*. Walnut Creek, CA: AltaMira Press.

Whitehouse, H. and Hodder, I. 2010. Modes of religiosity at Çatalhöyük. In I. Hodder (ed.) *Religion in the emergence of civilization: Çatalhöyük as a case study*, 122–145. New York: Cambridge University Press.

Whitehouse, H. and Martin, L. H. (eds) 2004. *Theorizing Religions Past: Archaeology, History, and Cognition*. Walnut Creek, CA: AltaMira Press.

Whitehouse, H., Mazzucato, C., Hodder, I. and Atkinson, Q. D. 2014. Modes of religiosity and the evolution of social complexity at Çatalhöyük. In I. Hodder (ed.) *Religion at Work in a Neolithic Society: Vital Matters*, 134–55. Cambridge University Press: Cambridge.

Whitehouse N. J., Schulting, R. J., McClatchie, M., Barratt, P., McLaughlin T. R., Bogaard, A., Colledge, S., Marchant, R., Gaffrey J., Bunting, M. J. 2014. Neolithic agriculture on the European western frontier: the boom and bust of early farming in Ireland. *Journal of Archaeological Science* 51, 181–205.

Wilde, W. R. 1849. *The beauties of the Boyne and the Blackwater*. Dublin. (Reprinted 2003 in Headford, Co. Galway by Kevin Duffy.)

Wilde, W. R. 1857. *Catalogue of the antiquities of stone, earthen and vegetable materials in the Museum of the Royal Irish Academy*. Dublin: M. H. Gill.

Wilson, J. and Berrow, S. 2oo6. *A Guide to the Identification of the Whales and Dolphin of Ireland*. Kilrush, Co. Clare: Published by the Irish Whale and Dolphin Group.

Woodman, P. 2000. Getting back to basics: transitions to farming in Ireland and Britain. In D. Price (ed.) *Europe's First Farmers*, 218–59. Cambridge: Cambridge University Press

Wood-Martin, W. G. 1888. *The Rude Stone Monuments of Ireland (Co. Sligo and the Island of Achill)*. Dublin: Hodges and Figgis.

Index

Numbers in italics denote pages with illustrations

Abbeyquarter, Co. Sligo 22
Achnacreebeag, Argyll 24
agriculture 7, 17, 18, 21–22, 26, 28, 29, 50–52, 53, 54, 62, 80, 111, 117, 137, 155
altered states of consciousness 40, 58–60, 63, 132, 157
ancestors 3, 27, 35, 39, 52, 59, 64, 65, 83, 94, 95, 130, 137, 156, 157
Anglesey 25, 72
Antrim, County 13, 23, 26, 113, 139
art, megalithic 5, 7, 8, 10, 11, 12, 13, 21, 41, 45–49, 61, 65, 95, 98–99, 107, 108, 109, 116, 118, 119–120, 125–132, 133, 136, 137, 138, 139, 140, 143, 145, 148, 149, 150, 152, 153, 154, 157, 158
    depictive 47, 94, 131
    entoptic 58–60, 132
    hache-charrue 88
    hidden 4–5, 108, 120–125, 121, 129–132
    incised 60, 61
    interpretation 46–47, 120
    motifs, range 45, 120, 131
    paint 38, 60, 145
    pick-dressing 4–5, 46, 47, 123, 128–130, 149
    'plastic' 47–48, 149
    relief 45, 89, 93
    rock art 149
    superimposition Plate 4, 47, 48, 48, 119, 120, 125
    techniques 45
    triple spiral 98–99
astronomical orientation 8, 21, 29, 43–44, 46, 54, 66–78, 95, 107, 117, 137, 143, 145, 147–148

Ballinacrad (Site G) Dowth, Co. Meath 100, 158
Ballintoy, Co. Antrim 23, 23–24
Baltinglass, Co. Wicklow 26, 45, 96, 97, 108, 137
Barclodiad y Gawres, Anglesey 87
Barnabrack, Co. Sligo 22
Barnasrahy, Co. Sligo 41
Bellah, Robert 155
Belmore, Co. Fermanagh 32, 36
Bergh, Stefan 142
Bloch, Maurice 155–156
boat, travel by 6, 28, 80, 84, 86, 92
bone, human 2, 3, 7, 26, 27, 28, 33, 34, 39, 41, 52, 53, 55, 101, 107, 108, 112, 137, 140, 153
boulder circle 12, 13, 19, 20, 20, 22, 23, 25, 30, 99, 143

Boyne, River *Plate 1*, 3, 6, 13, 32, 67, 79–84, 86, 93, 94,

Boyne Valley *see* Brú na Bóinne complex

Brady, Conor 86, 113

Bremore /Gormanstown, Co. Dublin 12, 139

Britain 21, 24, 25, 26, 28, 52, 80, 82, 97, 118, 137, 139, 150, 159

Broadsands, Devon 24, 26, 137

Bryn Celli Ddu, Anglesey 71, 73, 87

Bryn Yr Hen Bobl, Anglesey 87

Brú na Bóinne complex, Co. Meath 10, *11*, 16, 27, 32, 36, 45, 70, 79, 80, 94, 99, 101, 103, 113, 116, 117, 118, 119, 124, 139, 142, 149, 150–153 (*see also* individual sites, *e.g.* Knowth, Dowth)

Brück, Joanna 114

Burenhult, Göran 17

Cairn Dáithí, Co. Mayo 106

Camster Round, Caithness 40

Carn Ban, Isle of Arran 38, 39

Carns Hill East, Co. Sligo 105

Carns Hill West, Co. Sligo 97, 98, 105

Carrowkeel, Co. Sligo 10, *11*–12, 15, 32, *35*, 36, 41, 45, 99, 101, 103, 109, 111, 139, 140, 144–147, *146*, 148, 149, 152

    Cairn A 144

    Cairn B *42*, 140, 144, 145

    Cairn C 144

    Cairn D 144

    Cairn E 109, 153, 154

    Cairn F 36, 56, *56*, 108, 109, 144, 145

    Cairn G *35*, *57*, 71, *72*, 144, 145, *146*

    Cairn H *35*, 36, 87, *146*

    Cairn K *Plate 3*, 144, *146*

    Cairn L *146*

    Cairn M 41, 144

    Cairn N 41

    Cairn O 144, *146*

    Cairn P 144, *146*

    Heapstown Cairn 12, 13, 99, 105, 109, *110*, 140, 141, 145, 150

    Mullaghfarna *146*

Carrowmore, Co. Sligo *Preface*, 6, 12, 15, 16, 17–21, 22, 24, 25, 26, 27, 30, 36, 43, 45, 61, 87, 88, 99, 101, 103, 111, 112, 138, 139, 140, 142–144, 145, 147, 148, 149, 156

    Carrowmore 3: 13, 18, *20*

    Carrowmore 7: 87, 142, *143*

    Carrowmore 15: 88

    Carrowmore 51/Listoghil 12, 97, 140, 142–143

    Carrowmore 55A 18

    excavations 17–18, 19–21, 30

    Pins Project 2, 18–19

Carrowreagh, Co. Mayo 23

Cassen, Serge 88

Çatal Höyük, southern Anatolia 63, 116–117

chert 26

climate 3, 21, 29, 44, 50, 74, 111, 115, 139, 157, 159

Clogher Head, Co. Louth 84, *85*, 86, 93

Coffey, George 123

colour 38–39, 49, 75–76, 100, 128, 129

competitive construction 112

continental connections 1, 6–9, 93

Conwell, Eugene 15, 108, 147, 150

Cooney, Gabriel 117, 142

Cooney Lough, Co. Sligo 18

corbelled roofs 7, 13, 29, 36, 37, *37*, 38, 96, 123

Corcoran, Mary 86

crowds/gatherings 98, 112–115, 116, 118, 158

Cúil Irra peninsula, Co. Sligo 22, 71, 109, 140, 142

cultural historical archaeology 6, 16, 17

darkness 35, 55, 57, 58, 65, 73, 145

deposition, subterranean 52–53

Derrynahinch, Co. Kilkenny 106

diet 80–81, 111

Dowth, Co. Meath 10, 27, 70, 75, 80, 95, 98, 100, 105, 108, 128, 158

Drogheda, Co. Louth 81, 82, 84

Eliade, Mircea 51

Eliasson, Olafur *Plate 6*, 77

Enniscrone, Co. Sligo 22

Eochy's Cairn (Neale), Co. Mayo 105

Eogan, George 99, 115, 124, 132, 142

Eriksen, Palle 133, 134

Farranharpy, Co. Sligo 22

Fergusson, Samuel 123, 134

Finner, Co. Donegal 12

flint 26, 45, 52, 86, 113, 136

Fourknocks, Co. Meath 45, 87, 153–154

France, Brittany 1, 6–9, 24, 25, 38, 88, 94, 137

Fraser, Shannon 113, 142

Gavrinis, Brittany 7

grooved ware 152

Harbison, Peter 94, 110

Herity, Michael 87

Hodder, Ian 63

hunter-gatherers 16, 17, 50–52

Iberia/Spain 1, 7, 38, 118

Ibister, South Ronaldsay 88

Ingold, Timothy 76

invisible beings (spirits, deities) 27, 32, 44, 51, 52, 54, 55, 59, 62, 64, 65, 83, 115, 123, 130, 156, 157

Irish Sea 25, 87, 91, 93

Jones, Andrew 38, 39, 47

Keadeen, Co. Wicklow 100

kerbstones 13, 20, 24, 30, 45, 47, 48, 67, 84, 86, 96, 97, 98–99, 107, 108, 109, 120, 123, 125, 127, 133, 134, 136, 147, 148, 150, 151, 153 (*see also* Newgrange/kerbstones)

Kilmonaster, Co. Donegal 12, 32

Knockeiran/Rathnabo, Co. Wicklow 100

Knocklea, Co. Dublin 87

Knockma, Co. Galway 106

Knockmany, Co. Tyrone 32, 45

Knocknarea, Co. Sligo 22, 71, 109, 110, *143*, 145

Knockroe, Co. Kilkenny 38, 45, 70, 96, 97, 106–107

Knowth, Co. Meath 1, 3, 10, 27, 30, 33, 35, 38, 43, 45, 60, 80, 95, 97, 98, 99, 102, 105, 107, 115, 116, 119, 120, *122*, 124, 125, 129, 141, 142, 145, 149, 150–152, 158

    macehead (Knowth East) 102, *103*

    orthostat 45 (Knowth West) 47, *48*

    Site 1, eastern tomb 35, 60, 104

    Site 1, western tomb *Plate 7*, 36, 88–93, 109, 131

    Site 2: 151

    Site 4: 151

    Site 6: 41, *42*

    Site 13: 151

    Site 16: 151

Site 17: 41
Kogi, Columbia 58
Kong Svend's Høj passage tomb, Denmark 43

La Hougue Bie, Jersey 71
Leinster 99, 100, 113
Lemnaghbeg, Co. Antrim *Plate 2*, 23
Lewis-Williams, David 59
linear monuments 99–100, 107, 147, 158
Loughcrew, Co. Meath 10–11, 12, 15, 32, 36, 45, 99, 101, 103, 108, 113, 139, 142, 145, 147–150, 152
    Cairn B 41
    Cairn D 107–108, 147, 149, 150
    Cairn F 101, 148
    Cairn H *42*, 87, 148
    Cairn I *Plate 3*, 36, 40, 41, 56
    Cairn L 36, 37, 40, 41, *42*, 56, 102, 108, 109, 147, *148*, 149
    Cairn S 148, 149
    Cairn T Plate 3, 11, 37, 41, 70, 97, 98, 108, 147, 148, *148*, 149, 150
    Cairn V 149
    Cairn W 148
    Cairn X1, Patrickstown Hill 70, 148
    Thomastown 70, 148
Lough Dargan, Co. Sligo 18
Lynch, Ann 120
Lynch, Frances 6, 24, 25

Macalister, R. A. S. 15, 108, 144
Maeshowe, mainland Orkney 40, 70, 73
Magheracar, Co. Donegal 23
May, Susan 77
McCormick, Finbar 87
Millin Bay, Co. Down 45, 46, 153

Mitchell, Frank 32, 80
modes of religiosity 60–65
    imagistic 63–65, 116, 117, 130, 157
    doctrinal 62–64, 116–118, 158
Moroney, Anne Marie 75
Mourne Mountains, Co. Down 102

Newgrange *Plates 1 & 5*
    before Newgrange 4–6, 132–136
    boulders, under cairn 134
    cairn 5, 13, 36, 98, 120, 123, 132, 133, 134, 136, 159
    chamber 4, 7, 27, 36, 41, 47, 66–69, 73, 121, 123, 125, 128, 134
    construction stones, recycled 4, 124, 125, 126, 129, 132
    cursus 100, 158
    door-/closing stone 73
    east/right recess 41, *42*, 46, 102, *104*, 123, 125, *126*, 129
    entrance stone *see* kerbstones (K1)
    excavations 5, 17, 31, 80, 97, 102, 120, 122, 123, 132, 134, 136, 141
    granite and granodiorite 38, 84, *85*, 98, 102
    greywacke 84, 86, 129
    kerbstones: K1 (entrance stone) 45, 47, 97, 99, 127, *127*, 128, 131; K2 127; K4 120; K11 120; K13 120, *121*; K18 120; K21–47 120; K52 127, 131; K56-79; 120–121; K67 120, 127; K79 136; K95 133; K97 127
    materials, transportation of 4, 84, 85, 86, 87, 93, 113, 114, 115, 118, 152
    orthostats 67, 121, *122*, 123, 125, 128, 129, 134
    orthostat L19 *Plate 4*, 47, 121, *122*, 128, 130

passage 4, 35, 121, 122, 128, 133–134, *135*, 136
polity 113, 114, 118
plan and elevation *135*
platform (quartz) 97, 136
reconstruction, modern 17, 97, 147, 159
roof-box *Preface, Plates 5 & 8*, 45, 66, 68, 73, *74*, 122, 125, 127, 134, 136
Site B *Plate 1*
Site K 41, *42*
Site L 151
Site Z 41, *42*
spring (under passage) 134
turf mound 5, 81, 132–133, 136, 141
turves, within cairn 133, 135, 136
wall/façade 8, 38, 84, 97, 98, 134, 147
water grooves *Plate 8*, 4, 5

Ó Gibne, Claidhbh 86
O'Kelly, Claire 125, 128, 130, 131, 132
O'Kelly, M. J. 4, 17, 66, 68, 70, 80, 87, 102, 110, 120, 124, 128, 132, 133, 134, 153, 155, 159
O'Sullivan, Muiris 7, 38, 39, 47, 48, 59, 125
Orkney Islands 7, 8, 38, 40, 70, 72, 88, 152
Orokaiva, Papua New Guinea 58
otherworld 2–3, 53, 55, 87–88, 155–158

passage tombs in Ireland (*see also* Types 1, 2 & 3)
assemblage 100–105
balls, stone 8, 26, 39, 101, *101*, 102, 148
basins stones 102–104, *104*, 108, 116, 148, 151, 158

cairn 7, 20, 26, 29, 30, 34, 96, 98, 100, 105, 108, 157, 159
Carrowkeel ware 101
chamber, elaboration of 7, 8, 19, 29, 34, 36, 37, 41, 56, 96, 108
complexes 10, *14*, 45, 64, 112, 138, 140–153
passage 13, 20, 25, 29, 30, *31*, 34–36, 41, *42*, 43–44, 67, 68, 73, 96, *135*
pendants and beads 39, 101
pins, bone and antler 8, 18, *19*, 88, 101
platforms 12, 95, 97, 107, 136, 143
quantity and distribution 12–13
recesses 7, 36, 41, 46, 55, 56, 57, *57*, 64, 71, 104, 108, 116
sequence of development 6, 15–16, 17, 19, 111, 137–140
settings, stone 38, 98, 102, 110, 147, 150, 151
sillstones 35
standing stones 108, 109, 150
Phillips, Adrian 86
Point of Cott, Westray 88
Prendergast, Frank 70

quarrying 86, 115
quartz 8, 38, 39, 45, 73, 84, *85*, 93, 97, 98, 101, 107, 108, 136, 147, 150, 156 (*see also* note 6, Conclusion)
Queen Maeve's tomb 13, 22, 98, 105, 106, *106*, 109–110, 140, 141, *143*, 145, 150

Radiocarbon dating 16, 17, 18, 24, 26, 33, 81, 107, 108, 133, 136, 142, 143, 144, 147, 151 (*see also* note 8, Ch.5; note 35, Ch.7)
Red Mountain, Co. Meath *11*, 67
reincarnation/rebirth 53, 83, 94, 157, 158

Renfrew, Colin 1

right-hand preference 41–43, *42*, 49, 129

Robin, Guillaume 55, 94

Rockabill Island 84, *85*, 93

salmon 3, 79–84, 94

Scarre, Chris 7, 114

sea 2, 28, 34, 79, 80, 81, 82, 84–86, 88, 93, 137, 156

seeds 53, 157

Seefin, Co. Wicklow 32, 41, *42*, 45

Sess Kilgreen, Co. Tyrone 45

settlement/houses 21, 22, 28, 50, 111, *146*, 150, 156

Sevastopulo, George 84, 86

shamanism 40, 61–62, 132, 156

Sheemore, Co. Leitrim 12

Shee-Twohig 47, 149

shells, marine 86–88 (*see also* note 23, Ch. 5)

Sheridan, Alison 6, 25, 104

Slane, Co. Meath 86

Slieve Gullion, Co. Armagh *31*, 71, 102

Smohalla (Sioux prophet) 51

social elites 46, 75, 95, 112–114, 128, 158

solstice winter *Plate 5*, *Preface*, 9, 43, 44, 66–69, 70, 78, 82–83, 94, 98, 107, 117, 148, 158, 159

sound 40–41, 57

Stolze, Susan 111

Stout, Geraldine 86, 151

sun 3, 29, 41, 43, 44, 46, 53, 54, 66–69, 70–78, 81, 82, 83, 84, 94, 138, 157, 158, 159

Tara, Mound of the Hostages, Co. Meath 33, 100, 107, 153

Tilley, Christopher 39

Townleyhall II, Co. Meath *11*, 70

transcendental network *see* Bloch, Maurice

Turner, Victor 39

Type 1 phase 10–29, 23, 95, 138–139, 142, 150

    quantity and distribution of sites 22–27 (north-western group 22–23; north-eastern group 23–24; east & south 24; Britain 24–25)

    ritual 2–3, 20, 21, 27–28, 34, 156

Type 2 phase 29–49, 95, 104, 107, 116, 139, 145, 149, 151, 152

    quantity and distribution of sites 30, 32

    ritual 3, 29, 30, 33–36, 40, 43, 52–65, 71, 76, 104, 105, 116, 130, 138, 145, 157

Type 3 phase 95–115, *106*, *110*, 149

    quantity and distribution of sites 105–110, 145, 149

    ritual 3, 95, 96–100, 102, 105, 110–111, 112, 114, 115, 116–118, 130, 132, 138, 151, 156, 157, 158

Vallancey, Charles 46

Wales 8, 9, 25, 45, 71, 87, 112

Watson, Aaron 40

Westport House, Co. Mayo 23, 26

whale, possible humpback (and other) *Plate 7*, 88–94, *89*, *92*

Whitehouse, Harvey 62–63, 116, 118, 130

Whittle, Alasdair 52, 107

Wicklow Mountains 13, 84, *85*

Wilde, William *106*, 124

Wood-Martin, William 15, 16

Plate 1. Newgrange from the south with Site B in the foreground (Ken Williams).

Plate 2. Lemnaghbeg Type 1 passage tomb, Co. Antrim (Author).

Plate 3. Above: Cairn I, Loughcrew with Cairn T in the distance (Author). Below: Cairn K, Carrowkeel (Ken Williams).

Plate 4. Orthostat L19, Newgrange (Ken Williams).

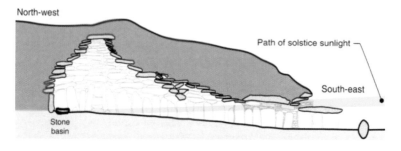

Plate 5. Above: Winter solstice sunlight entering Newgrange (Ken Williams).
Below: Path of solstice light (Stout and Stout, 2008, fig. 29).

Plate 6. 'The Weather Project', Olafur Eliasson (Courtesy of the Tate Modern).

Plate 7. Knowth West chamber art (Ken Williams).

Plate 8. Above: Hidden art on roof-box 'back corbel', Newgrange (Author).
Below: Deeply carved rainwater groove on Roofslab 3 above the passage at
Newgrange (Author).